MW00395594

The Transition from Sales and Operations Planning to Integrated Business Planning

*Moving from Fundamental Demand
and Supply Balancing to Strategic Management*

By George E. Palmatier with Colleen Crum
Oliver Wight

Published by Oliver Wight International
292 Main Street
New London, NH 03257
www.oliverwight.com

ISBN: 978-1-4575-1825-6

This book is printed on acid-free paper.

Printed in the United States of America

TABLE OF CONTENTS

This book is dedicated to Valerie Kramer and to Jerry Crum, two people whose lives affected far more people than they could ever imagine. Thank you, Valerie and Jerry.

By Torkel Rhenman, Chief Executive Officer, Lhoist Group

I am pleased that this book on Integrated Business Planning has been written. Every executive who thinks he or she has control of their business should read this book.

While I was an executive of a business at DuPont in the early 1990s, Oliver Wight Americas was engaged to assess our Sales and Operations Planning process. I looked forward to the assessment because I believed our process was very good.

George Palmatier of Oliver Wight took me aside after reviewing our process. In a very provocative and candid way, he pointed out what I was missing as the business leader by not having all functions aligned to one plan and by not being able to see gaps in the performance of the business.

George convinced me that my view of Sales and Operations Planning was too narrow. We viewed S&OP as mostly a near-term process for balancing demand and supply. George emphasized that our business needed a process for integrating *all* functions and ensuring that *all* plans were aligned and tied to strategy.

As a business leader, here's what I found so compelling about Integrated Business Planning:

- It is so logical, and it truly integrates the financial plan, the financial forecast outlook, sales and marketing plans, and operations plans.
- It links tactical plans to the execution of strategy and provides the means to continually challenge the strategy, rather than continuing to rely on an old and irrelevant strategy as market conditions change.
- It gives management teams greater confidence in making the decision to change plans as market and economic conditions change – because the planning numbers and projections are updated and vetted every month.
- It is an effective leadership process whether the business is mature, a startup, or a turnaround.

DuPont ended up requiring that all of its businesses implement what was named DuPont Integrated Business Management (DIBM), DuPont's name for Integrated Business Planning. The only other mandatory process at DuPont is Six Sigma. That's how important DIBM was to the health of DuPont.

In my final leadership position at DuPont, I served as the chief executive for a turnaround business. By the time I came to the company, I had three Integrated Business Planning implementations under my belt and could not imagine running a business without the IBP process.

I used Integrated Business Planning to bring the entire executive team together to focus on delivering the turnaround. Here's what we accomplished over the course of four years:

- Reduced working capital by 30 percent
- Improved forecast accuracy at the item and ship-to level from 50 percent to 70 percent
- Increased company pretax operating income by five times
- Improved the growth rate of this specialty chemical business from 3 to 4 percent per year to more than 10 percent per year
- Increased the accuracy of our financial plan from being highly inaccurate ($\pm$100 percent) to being highly predictable ($\pm$15 percent).
- Set financial and operational performance records for multiple years

In implementing Integrated Business Planning, I became a better business leader. Most business leaders like to experiment and develop their own processes, which they strive to continually perfect. With Integrated Business Planning, the process has already been perfected. Instead of experimenting, I was able to use IBP to more efficiently tie together strategy and execution and drive improved business performance.

We trusted the plan numbers and projections because we updated them every month. As a result, we did not consume huge amounts of time debating whether the numbers were accurate; we knew the numbers were as close to being accurate as possible. This gave the leadership team the time to focus on our strategy and tactics, given the changes in market conditions that were either occurring or were expected to occur.

I also used the integrated planning process as the means to create a culture of self-awareness where we could be safely self-critical of our functional and business performance. The leadership team set targets each year for what we wanted our Integrated Business Planning process to do for the business. This effort included identifying how much to improve forecast accuracy each year. Each year, we identified the volume growth for certain business segments. We also agreed upon the target for on-time delivery performance each year.

We monitored performance through the monthly Integrated Business Planning process. Discussions focused on how to make the improvements happen. For example, we focused on how we needed to invest in tools and training to enable our people to achieve the targets. We found that to be successful, we needed a solid demand plan. We invested in training the sales force and providing them with tools to do a better job. The sales team went from not being engaged in the process to being strongly involved in the process. Their involvement accelerated the results we were able to achieve.

Along the way, I learned that when implementing Integrated Business Planning, success starts with the business leader's personal commitment to the process. The business leader must be one step ahead of the rest of the executive team to push and prod for continuous improvement.

In singing the praises of Integrated Business Planning, I don't want to leave you with the impression that implementing it is easy. It is not, and that's why the business leader needs to be committed and personally involved. Initially, the organization sees that implementing IBP is extra work, especially as the IBP process begins to replace other processes. This extra burden gradually diminishes. As the well-structured, integrated process replaces those old informal processes that are not integrated, the workload eases.

When the workload diminishes and the integrated, well-structured process becomes dominant, the organization becomes much more focused. The strategy and tactics are well understood, including how they tie together. The expectations for outcomes, including financial performance, are clear. Rather than arguing about whose numbers are right, the people supporting each function and the management team focus on meeting the expectations of the business and marketplace.

Why I like this book on Integrated Business Planning is that it distinguishes the difference between Sales and Operations Planning and Integrated Business Planning. It also explains the integration of product portfolio management and financial planning and management. It explains the structure of Integrated Business Planning in a way that is logical and easy to understand.

I very much believe in three key things in running a business; that is, strategy, execution, and people. Integrated Business Planning is a fantastic process for tying all three together. I have implemented Integrated Business Planning four times in my career, and, in every case, it was a vital part of the business transformation.

In the writing of this book, and our other books, on variations and themes of integrated management processes, we have been extremely fortunate to draw upon the experiences of our many clients and our associates in the Oliver Wight companies. Over the past couple of decades, the integration of management processes has become more widespread, and the experiences in doing so are becoming richer and deeper.

The integrated management process of Sales and Operations Planning has continued to mature into something greater than originally envisioned; that is, Integrated Business Planning. As this maturation has occurred, we have had the opportunity to share our experiences with numerous clients and Oliver Wight team members. It is our pleasure to share this common body of knowledge with our readers.

In writing this book, we truly appreciate the reviews and comments made by Dennis Groves, Liam Harrington, Donald McNaughton, Mike Reed, Les Brookes, and Andrew Purton of the Oliver Wight organization. Their input has helped to improve the content and clarity of the material.

We extend hearty gratitude to Anne Hilton, Stephanie Willett, Karen DeMayo, and Susan Hansen in our Oliver Wight corporate office for their assistance in producing the book.

We also wish to thank our clients and fellow associates for their continued support to mature Integrated Business Planning. Their generosity in sharing their experiences is increasing the body of knowledge of how business leaders are managing their companies with fully integrated, executive teamwork.

George E. Palmatier, an Oliver Wight Americas principal, has assisted many companies that make everything from soup to satellites in implementing integrated management processes. He is recognized as an expert on Sales and Operations Planning, Integrated Business Planning, and Demand Management as well as ERP, Integrated Supply Chain Management, and Integrated Product Development (IPD). George works with clients to formalize and assimilate their strategic plans into a unified business management process, Integrated Business Planning. With twenty years of experience in sales, marketing, strategic planning, and general management, George has a thorough knowledge of how to achieve sustained results improving business performance. During his 11 years as vice president of sales and marketing at Bently Nevada Corporation (now part of General Electric), George was responsible for bringing the sales and marketing departments into a well-orchestrated business management process. Bently Nevada was one of the pioneers in developing and implementing Sales and Operations Planning using it as a truly integrated management process. In addition to his many white papers, George has authored or co-authored three books: *The Marketing Edge, Enterprise Sales and Operations Planning,* and *Demand Management Best Practices.* He is also a member of The Council of Supply Chain Management Professionals. George speaks frequently at association meetings and conferences as well as teaches Integrated Business Planning classes for Oliver Wight in both public and private settings.

Colleen "Coco" Crum, a principal with Oliver Wight Americas, is considered a thought leader and innovator in Demand Management, Integrated Business Planning, and change management. She has helped develop methodologies that enable companies to successfully implement Integrated Business Planning and Demand Management to achieve quick time to financial benefit. She has assisted companies across the manufacturing spectrum, including chemicals, consumer goods, food and beverage, electronics, biotechnology, and aerospace and defense. In addition to authoring many white papers, Coco has co-authored three books: *Enterprise Sales and Operations Planning, Demand Management Best Practices,* and *Supply Chain Collaboration.* She also participated in the development of a best practice model for grocery supply chain replenishment, which resulted in the publication of a book on Continuous Replenishment by Canadian food industry trade groups. She is a frequent speaker at conferences and instructs the Oliver Wight Demand Management Course.

The Oliver Wight companies is a team of distinguished, seasoned coaches and educators on integrated business processes, such as Integrated Business Planning, Demand Management, and Integrated Planning and Control. Our coaches and educators have broad industry experience and a steadfast commitment to help our clients achieve their business goals. We don't just help organizations improve; we make sure they achieve business results that last.

Using our integrated approach to improvement and change management, we are dedicated to helping clients create value in their organizations. Here are examples of value that our clients report:

- Increases in sales revenue and market share
- Improved operating margins
- Development of new and more competitive products
- Improvement in cash flow
- Increases in return on assets

This story is an extension of the book *Enterprise Sales and Operations Planning*. It describes how a fictional company, Global Products and Services, Inc., continues to evolve Sales and Operations Planning into Integrated Business Planning.

In telling this story, the authors assume that the reader has a basic understanding of the integrated management process known as Sales and Operations Planning. If the reader has not already read *Enterprise Sales and Operations Planning*, the authors encourage you to do so. It will help you to understand how the management team at Global Products and Services, Inc., has reached this point - in both improving business performance and needing to continue to evolve the business management process.

The Company:

Global Products and Services, Inc., a multi-divisional, global company, headquartered in the USA, and serving multiple markets with a variety of products and services.

The Players:

Jack Baxter ....President, Global Products and Services, Inc

Janis Novak ....Corporate Controller

Ross Peterson ....Lead Consultant, Effective Management, Inc.

Mark Ryan ....General Manager, Executive Vice President, Aerospace Business Unit

Cheryl Ryan ....Mark's wife

Chad Ryan ....Mark and Cheryl's son

Sheri Waterman...........Administrative Assistant for Mark Ryan

Taylor Jackson ....Vice President Strategic Planning, Global Products and Services, Inc.

Bailey Madison.............Vice President Supply Chain Management, Global P & S, Inc.

Nolan Justin ....Corporate Information Technology Director, Global P & S, Inc.

Bill Williams ....Project Coordinator

Tim Osborne...............Demand Planning Process Leader

Just another morning?

Jack Baxter, President of Global Products and Services, Inc., rolls out of bed. It is 4:30 in the morning.

Jack has been a "morning person" for about five years. Jack brushes his teeth and then proceeds to exercise and stretch for twenty minutes. This routine is part of his concerted effort to manage his physical health and weight, which seems to get more difficult every year. He continues his morning routine with meditation to help keep his mind and spirit positive. Finally, he finishes with a brisk shower, dresses, and is ready for another day.

Jack is in Denver, Colorado, and has scheduled a breakfast meeting this morning with his long-time friend and associate, Mark Ryan. Mark has been running the Aerospace business unit that Global Products and Services acquired seven years ago, and the business has been doing well, even during tough economic times. Prior to Mark's current assignment, Jack made Mark responsible for implementing Sales and Operations Planning (S&OP) in eight Global Products and Services, Inc., business units around the world.

As Jack drives to the Aerospace business unit offices, he pauses to consider the impact that Sales and Operations Planning has had on the company. It has proven to be the most significant company-wide initiative that Global Products and Services, Inc. has ever undertaken. All eight business units have significantly improved their business performance as a result of changing the way the businesses were managed. Some business units achieved greater results than others; but all eight divisions, as well as the recent acquisition, effectively use the Sales and Operations Planning process.

While the processes are not perfect in each business unit, the business units align and synchronize all the business functions internally and are more effectively connecting externally with customers and markets.

That's no small achievement, Jack says to himself. Yet, he has a nagging worry. The performance of some business units appears to have stagnated and, Jack fears, their Sales and Operations Planning processes may have atrophied. At the same time, some of the other business units have continued to improve their Sales and Operations Planning processes and continue to meet or exceed their business goals and targets.

Why have some business units atrophied and others have not? Jack suspects the variation in performance is caused, in part, by management changes, promotions, and turnover, which is just normal business life. Additional stressors are changes in customers and markets, particularly coming out of the Great Recession.

It seems to Jack that the business units that more fully embraced Sales and Operations Planning as an integrated business management process have been more adaptable to both internal and external changes. As a result, they have been the top-performing business units in the company.

Jack pulls into the parking lot. He wonders whether Mark will be willing to take on another assignment. He knows Mark has been comfortable in Colorado. His current job does not require that he travel nonstop, and Jack knows Mark and his wife, Cheryl, have enjoyed having more time together.

Jack remains in the car for a few minutes, thinking about how he might convince Mark to accept this new assignment. He hopes that Mark appreciates Jack's confidence in him. Jack knows that Mark is the right person for the task he has in mind for him. He will need to reassure Mark that he won't have to move from Colorado. Mark's son, Chad, is living in Durango, which is just a few hours' drive from Denver, close enough for the family to see each other at least every few weeks. Jack will also reassure Mark that he will have plenty of support. It won't be like starting all over again. Bailey Madison, the corporate Vice President of Supply Chain Management, will be a great asset and can carry a good deal of the load for Jack's new initiative.

As Jack walks into the building, he hopes that Mark will jump at the opportunity to help the company once again.

Chapter 1

The Proposition

MARK RYAN, THE EXECUTIVE VICE President of the Aerospace business unit, answers his emails while waiting for Jack to arrive. He looks out the window at the Colorado Rockies. The morning sun slants across the eastern slopes. It is a beautiful sight and is one of the main reasons that he and Cheryl were delighted to make Colorado their home. He also knows it is one of the main reasons their son, Chad, has elected to spend at least a couple of years working in Colorado.

Mark laughs at himself. Chad's girlfriend might have been an influence, too. He hopes, though, that Chad will decide sometime in the near future to pursue an MBA at a well-known school with the same enthusiasm that he and his girlfriend have pursued skiing, backpacking, and fishing.

Who knows, maybe earning his MBA will make it possible for Chad to marry and have a few children of his own. Now, Mark really chuckles at himself. Are he and Cheryl *really* ready to be grandparents? Boom-Pa and Nana?

Thank heavens, Sheri Waterman interrupts Mark's reverie. "Jack's just stepped out of his car. Will you need anything from me for the meeting?" she asks.

Sheri has been a blessing to Mark. She chose to move with him to the Aerospace business after Global Products and Services acquired the company seven years ago. Changing jobs did not require that Sheri move from Denver. It just extended her drive to work by twenty minutes, but Sheri never complains, even during snowstorms.

Just as Mark starts to tell Sheri that he won't need anything from her during the meeting, Jack taps Sheri on the shoulder.

"Good morning, Sheri and Mark. What a beautiful morning!"

Mark springs up from his chair and extends his hand to Jack. "And a good morning to you, Jack," he says. "I trust you had uneventful travels and a good night's sleep."

Sheri excuses herself, and Jack and Mark eyeball one another.

"We have a lot to discuss, Mark," Jack says. "Are you ready to roll up your sleeves and get to work?"

Mark nods his head. "Let's go to the cafeteria and get some coffee. We can talk there," he says.

Mark and Jack stop by Sheri's desk on the way to the cafeteria. "Sheri, I will be tied up most of the morning. I'll return calls just before lunch," he says.

Sheri nods and says, "Remember, you have your staff meeting at 1:00 this afternoon."

As Mark and Jack walk down the hall to the cafeteria, Mark clasps Jack's shoulder and says, "What's up, big man. I have a feeling this is not a social call."

Jack laughs. "You always have been good at reading me. I'm dying for a cup of coffee. Let's sit by that big picture window and catch up on the family news. Then we can talk about what brings me to town."

Mark tells Jack of his morning reverie about becoming a grandfather. Jack laughs out loud.

"Donna and I went through the same thing a few years back," he said. "It's normal. On the one hand, what's better than grandchildren! On the other hand, will people look at you as being old!"

They stare out the window at the Rocky Mountains, alone in their thoughts for a few moments. Then, Jack shifts gears.

"Mark, let's get to the primary reason why I am here. As you know, I have continued to maintain contact with Ross Peterson. Ross is a coach and advisor from the consulting firm, Effective Management, Inc."

"How is Ross?" Mark asks. "We talk from time to time, but it's been six months or so since our last conversation."

"He's just fine. Same old Ross," Jack says. "I called Ross because I'm concerned that the performance of some of our business units is not improving, and I'm worried that their S&OP processes have stagnated. I wanted his take on the situation."

"I hope you weren't concerned about my Aerospace business unit," Mark replies.

Jack shakes his head. "No, Mark. The Aerospace business unit continues to be a top performer, thanks to your leadership and management skills. But we did talk about you."

Without hesitating, Jack launches into his proposition.

"Mark, I want you to take another assignment. I want you to review the S&OP processes in the other business units, using Ross Peterson of Effective Management and members of his team as a resource. After talking with Ross, I'm sure that we are missing some key business benefits from S&OP in some of the business units."

Mark does not reply immediately. He rubs his chin and stares out the window. After a few moments, he turns back to Jack.

"I'm glad that you are happy with the Aerospace business unit's performance," he says. "It's hard to believe that it's been seven years since we acquired the business. It seems like only yesterday that you had me work with Ross to lead the implementation of S&OP in all the business units. But here's what I don't understand. Why me this time? Shouldn't someone else be given the chance to tune up the S&OP processes in the business units?"

Jack is ready for Mark's question and quickly responds.

"Mark, you are clearly the best choice. You have the best knowledge of S&OP in all of Global Products. You gained this knowledge by leading the original implementation at the Universal Products business unit and from operating the process as General Manager of the Aerospace division. You used S&OP as your management process to run both businesses. And you achieved top-notch business results, I might add. What we need now goes beyond a tune-up."

Sheri walks into the cafeteria to refill her coffee cup. She sees Mark and Jack across the cafeteria, heads bent, deep in conversation. Jack is telling Mark of his conversation with Ross Peterson. Sales and Operations Planning has evolved into more than just balancing demand, supply, and inventory. Companies are making great gains by evolving Sales and Operations Planning into an industry best practice for strategic management. Some leading companies have given the process a new name to differentiate it from what they have done in the past. The most common name now being used is Integrated Business Planning, or IBP.

"Jack, we already use the S&OP process as a strategic management process, at least in the Aerospace and Universal Products business units," Mark says. "So what's the big deal?"

"That's true," Jack replies. "But I think both business units are ahead of the curve, and that's why I need you now to lead the effort in reviewing and rejuvenating S&OP in all of the business units, plus at the corporate level. With your help, we can learn something to help us perform better."

"How does this effort fit with the rumors I've heard about Bailey Madison heading up an enterprise performance initiative?" Mark asks. "Are we talking about the same initiative?"

"I envision the two of you working closely together," Jack replies. "You will need to make sure that the strategic management process is connected to execution. That means the Integrated Business Planning process must be integrated with the detailed execution processes. You'll have the aggregate planning process, the IBP process. Bailey will focus on the detailed execution processes, or Integrated Supply Chain Management, and how the aggregate plans will be translated into detailed planning and control."

Jack pauses to make sure Mark is following what he has said. Mark nods to show he understands.

Jack continues. "Ross tells me that companies squander opportunities by not making sure they are aligned and synchronized at the execution level as well as at the leadership level. I think it's a weakness we may have in many of the business units."

Mark ponders Jack's remark for a moment, then asks, "Does this detailed planning and control work include the collaborative planning efforts with our customers and suppliers, or just our suppliers?"

Jack shrugs his shoulders. "I honestly don't know at this point," he says. "What I do know is that companies that do Sales and Operations Planning well are moving toward Integrated Business Planning. I also know that greater benefits are achieved when the leadership management process is connected to execution through the detailed planning and control process, more specifically, with Integrated Supply Chain Management. I also know that we have some key customers asking us to collaborate with them and that we are already attempting to collaborate with key suppliers. Beyond that, I just don't know; but that's why I want you and Bailey to work together."

"So, Jack, where is all this information coming from? Is this all from Ross?"

"A lot of the clarity is coming from Ross, yes. But Bailey has been doing some discovery as well. She's been talking to both customers and suppliers. I've also been talking with a number of executives in other companies, and Ross has shared the results of a number of independent surveys that have come out on Sales and Operations Planning in recent years."

Jack pauses and waves a greeting at the Aerospace division controller before returning his attention to Mark. "I am convinced that we have a significant opportunity to continue to improve corporate performance through improving and enhancing Sales and Operations Planning. It is key to integrate our executive management process with our planning and control processes, and we must better connect with both customers and suppliers. Mark, will you take on this initiative?"

Mark does not answer right away, and Jack does not expect him to do so. He respects Mark because he is thoughtful and able to think things through without becoming paralyzed. He also knows that once Mark makes a commitment, he will see it through to the end.

Mark's mind goes back in time. He truly enjoyed leading the Sales and Operations Planning project a few years ago, but the travel was the downside. With Jack's latest proposition, Mark knows it means more travel.

The real dilemma for Mark, however, will be giving up his current role, at least for some period of time, as general manager of the Aerospace business unit. He can't see it working any other way. An upside will be working with Bailey Madison; he knows that they will make a good team. It will also be good to work with Ross Peterson again. Ross always brings a lot of experience and the most current thinking in the industry. He is sure that Ross will be an invaluable mentor and coach, just like he was during the previous project.

Mark pushes from the table and leans back in his chair. Here come the questions, Jack says to himself.

True to form, Mark turns his questions into statements, rapid fire, seeking Jack's confirmation. "I assume that you will be the corporate executive sponsor, and I can call upon you if I have reluctant general managers in the other business units?"

Jack nods in agreement.

"I assume you will give me Ross Peterson and Effective Management, Inc. as a resource for education and coaching, as we did before."

Jack again nods in agreement.

"I won't be able to do my current job as the general manager of Aerospace and do the project leadership work on this initiative. So, someone will have to be named as interim GM until the project is complete. Is that correct? Or do you see me giving up this GM role completely?"

Jack knew this question would be on the table, and he has already thought through his answer. "Mark, I plan on naming an interim GM, with your concurrence, until we get a better handle on how much work is involved and how long it will take for this project. We will need to work with Ross to better define the work and the schedule. I know there is a diagnostic phase to the work, much like we did when we first implemented Sales and Operations Planning. After that phase, we will discuss the GM role again. I know, between the two of us, we can identify an interim GM until the first phase is completed."

Jack thinks the timing is right to launch into his "big speech," to state his expectations and assure Mark that he will remain a valued leader of the company after the initiative is completed.

"Mark, the potential benefits to the corporation are truly significant if we can integrate our executive management processes with the detailed planning and control processes in all of the business units. This is not a job to be left to someone we are training to promote to an executive-level position. We need an executive to lead the process, someone who is well regarded and has a good track record. Someone like you, Mark. There is no question in my mind that leading this project is the best use of your skills and experience for the future of Global Products and Services, Inc. We've done this before. And, as before, I will make sure it is worth your while to lead this effort. When the project is completed, you will have a key role in Global Products and Services, Inc. You will either return as GM of the Aerospace business unit, or you will be given another opportunity in a key role. We will make the decision together."

Jack pauses for a moment. He sees that Mark is looking at him intently. Jack decides to preempt Mark's next question, veiled as a statement.

"Mark, I know that your next question will be about location. There is no need to relocate to lead this project. As before, the project will entail a lot of travel. But I have to be honest with you. Once this project is done, if you are no longer general manager of the Aerospace business, I can't guarantee that the next assignment will be in Colorado."

Jack stands up and stretches. "I don't expect an answer today. I am sure you will want to talk to Cheryl before making a decision."

Mark is on his feet, looking at his watch, mindful that he has a staff meeting at one o'clock. It is noon. He has time to call Cheryl. She loves Colorado and being near Chad, but she is also always up for an adventure.

"Okay, Jack. I think I understand the business issue and the opportunity for me to be of service to Global Products on this project. I do want to talk to Cheryl first."

Jack smiles, liking Mark's positive signals. "I knew that would be the case. I planned another engagement this evening so you could be free to talk with Cheryl. Why don't you take her out to dinner, on the company? You and I can go over the details tomorrow morning."

Mark shook his head at his boss; same old Jack. "I did not say 'yes' yet, Jack," Mark declares.

Jack shrugs his shoulders. Busted. He decides contrition is appropriate.

"I know Cheryl needs to be in agreement, Mark, but I am also sure you will do the right thing. Let's get together first thing in the morning. I plan to fly out around noon tomorrow."

Chapter 2

The First Step

IT IS A WEEK LATER, and Mark and his team are not wasting time getting started. As he awaits the start of the initial team session at a conveniently located hotel, Mark thinks back to all that has occurred in just seven days.

He smiles as he thinks about how Jack, once again, talked him into leading a major company initiative. Mark knew that Cheryl would support this opportunity, and she did not disappoint him. She readily admitted that she really likes Colorado, but she also likes opportunities for her family "to stretch our wings," as she described it over the dinner that Jack so generously bought. One thing Mark loves about Cheryl is her "sense of adventure," his words, or "restless nature," Cheryl's words.

During their dinner, Cheryl observed that they had been in one place in Colorado longer than any other time in Mark's career. "Maybe this opportunity is good timing for us," Cheryl said. "We can seek new challenges in new places."

Things came together nicely at Global Products and Services, too. Not surprisingly, Jack asked Bailey Madison to call Mark and encourage Mark to take the project leadership role. They talked about how the project was an integration effort, linking Strategic Management with detailed Integrated Planning and Control. They decided to propose to Jack that they be joint leaders. Mark would lead the Integrated Business Planning effort, and Bailey would lead the detailed integrated planning and control and supply chain collaboration effort. Jack was delighted with their proposal.

Mark called Ross Peterson of Effective Management, Inc. shortly after accepting the project leadership role for the Integrated Business Planning effort. Ross expected the call; Jack had already asked him to be prepared to once again work with Mark in this effort.

Ross and Mark were happy to be working together again. They had stayed in touch over the years, exchanging both professional and family news as well as jokes that make the rounds on email.

In their most recent phone conversation, they discussed who should be on the project core team. Ross recommended that he get people from corporate representing finance, information technology, and corporate strategy and/or marketing. He further advised that these corporate representatives needed to be strong players with the ability to help in the initial scoping effort. Mark and Bailey would represent operations management. Mark knew, from his previous project, he would need an administrative assistant as well.

Since each of the Global Products and Services divisions is largely independent with few shared resources, Mark decided a large central project team was not necessary. Ross observed that the more shared facilities and resources a company has, the more important it is that all the functions and business units be represented on the central project team. But, given that each division at Global Products and Services operates essentially as an independent business, a large central team was not necessary, at least initially.

Mark glances down at his notepad where he has written the names of the core team members:

Mark Ryan – Corporate Project Leader for Integrated Business Planning
Bailey Madison – Corporate Vice President, Supply Chain Management, and Corporate Project Leader for Integrated Planning and Control and Supply Chain Optimization
Taylor Jackson – Corporate Vice President, Strategic Planning
Janis Novak – Corporate Controller (promoted recently from Controller for the Universal Products division)
Nolan Justin – Information Technology Director
Bill Williams – Administrative Project Coordinator

Having led these projects before and having worked with Effective Management, Inc. in doing so, Mark knew that the core team would need a common level of understanding of the best practice principles and the approach to the project. He had arranged for Ross Peterson to lead a one-day education and workshop session to bring everyone up to speed.

Mark looks at his watch. He expects Ross to arrive in one hour for the education session. Mark hasn't seen Ross in several years. He wonders if Ross has a little more gray hair, like Mark now has.

He thinks about his last conversation with Ross. He was genuinely pleased to have an opportunity to work with Global Products and Services, Inc., once again. He and his Effective Management, Inc. team worked so well together on the Sales and Operations Planning implementation. Ross told Mark how he connected with Jack again and what spurred their conversation toward Integrated Business Planning.

Jack had gone to a baseball game with Paul, a long-time friend, who was the CEO of a fast-moving, consumer goods company. Between beers, hot dogs, and watching out for foul balls slicing toward their box seats, Jack and his friend, Paul, swapped stories about their respective companies. Paul told Jack how he had "supercharged" his Sales and Operations Planning process and how the company's performance improved by doing so. Jack had asked whether they used outside help in making the improvements. It turned out that Paul's company used Effective Management, Inc., although another trusted adviser and coach worked with Paul's company.

The next day, Jack called Ross, and they scheduled a meeting at corporate headquarters for Ross to brief Jack on how to supercharge the Sales and Operations Planning process. Ross laughed at the description. "We've been calling it a transition or evolution to Integrated Business Planning," he said. "But 'supercharged' is a much sexier description!"

What struck Jack most about Integrated Business Planning was the comparison in performance achieved by companies that operate the integrated management process well versus companies that operate the process in a mediocre manner. Ross showed Jack the following chart from a research firm. (See Figure 1.)

	Reported % Improvement Ranges
Revenue Growth	10-31%
Gross Margin	25-29%
Demand Plan Accuracy	18-43%
On-Time Delivery In Full	10-50%
Order Fill Rate	29-34%
Perfect Order	22-30%
Customer Satisfaction	29-39%
Inventory Turns	24-28%
Inventory Value	33-37%
Inventory Reduction	18-46%
Safety Stock Reduction	11-45%
Working Capital	25-30%
Asset Utilization	32-49%
Increased Productivity	30-45%
Return on Assets	24-30%

Sources: Oliver Wight International, Aberdeen,
AMR, and Ventana Research

Figure 1   Reported Improvements as a Result of Integrated Business Planning
(Copyright Oliver Wight International. Reproduced with permission.)

Jack found it interesting to learn the types of business results that companies achieve by operating Sales and Operations Planning well. The benefits are not just in cost improvements, which even companies with a mediocre Sales and Operations Planning process typically achieve. Companies that have effective Integrated Business Planning processes exceed those benefits. They also realize increased top-line sales revenue and market share. Jack hadn't thought of utilizing Sales and Operations Planning to drive improvements in sales revenue and market share.

Ross explained how companies were able to get those top-line improvements by contrasting the primary difference between companies that only achieved cost savings and those companies that also achieved increased sales and market share. It turns out that companies with both bottom-line and top-line gains did not solely focus the Sales and Operations Planning process on aligning demand, supply, and inventory. They used Sales and Operations Planning as a strategic management process as well.

This approach was not something that Jack had thought about before, but he had often lamented as to how difficult it was to ensure that the company's strategies were well executed. As Ross explained, the executive leaders of many companies were now using Sales and Operations Planning as a monthly management review of progress toward strategic goals and a review of strategic initiatives. There are several advantages in doing so. Increased management attention keeps the strategies top of mind. Sales and Operations Planning provides better visibility of the future and enables executive teams to adjust plans as conditions change.

It is a natural extension of Sales and Operations Planning to validate whether the latest projections and plans are aligned and synchronized with the company's strategies. If they are not, one or the other requires adjustment. In the end, companies that incorporate Strategic Management into the Sales and Operations Planning process improve execution because of the amount of attention and the actions taken to ensure that the strategies are executed. That's what drives improved business top-line performance improvements.

Ross recalled to Mark how surprised Jack was to find that the basic Sales and Operations Planning model had changed relatively little over the years. (See Figure 2.) Like most models, the Integrated Business Planning model does not capture the greatest change that occurs when companies transition from Sales and Operations Planning. The greatest change was in leadership and management *thinking*.

Jack described the shift in thinking as moving from short-term reactive management to longer-term strategic thinking and strategic management. Ross warned that this change may seem simple, but moving to strategic thinking is often the hardest part for an executive team.

Ross shared that one characteristic of companies that begin to use the monthly Sales and Operations Planning process for strategic management is that considerably more attention is paid to the Product Management Review in the monthly process. Since changes in strategy often drive changes in value propositions and product portfolios, this area receives much more of management's attention versus simply making sure that demand, supply, and inventory are in balance. Often, support processes like "stage and gate" reviews need to be implemented or shored up.

Following his conversation with Ross, Mark asked Bill Williams, the project integration leader, to set up an offsite meeting for the small, but high-powered

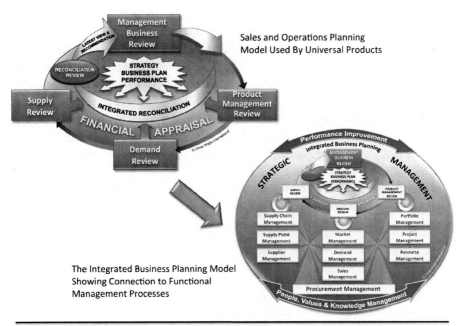

Sales and Operations Planning
Model Used By Universal Products

The Integrated Business Planning Model
Showing Connection to Functional
Management Processes

Figure 2 Aggregate Planning Models (Copyright Oliver Wight International. Reproduced with permission.)

central project team. One purpose of the meeting is to gain a common understanding of Sales and Operations Planning and its evolution into Integrated Business Planning. The other purpose is to discuss the implementation of the project in general. Ross will lead the one-day session.

Mark talked with Jack and Bailey. They agreed that the support required for each individual business division would not be determined in the session. The knowledge gained and the discussions in the session will help in identifying the right project team leaders in each division. The team members will, most likely, vary division by division, depending upon the diagnostic review conducted on the current state of each individual S&OP process.

Jack called each of the people who are expected to participate in the session facilitated by Ross. Travel to Japan prevented Jack from attending the session, which was unfortunate, but Jack did not want the process delayed because of him. In his phone call to each person, he conveyed quite convincingly the importance of the project. He told each team member that he championed the project and took it very seriously. He asked each team member to take the project equally seriously; company business performance was dependent upon their leadership of this project.

Mark looks up as the front doors of the hotel create a draft of cool air in the lobby. Bill and Ross have arrived at the hotel at the same time, ninety minutes early, to make sure the room is set up. Mark likes the location. It is close to the office, yet gets people away from day-to-day work so they can concentrate on the education session. All he is asking of team members at this time is one full day's attention.

Ross, Bill, and Mark greet one another and walk down the hall to the meeting room. They are happy that the room has been set up with tables in a u-shape, which will facilitate discussion. Ross reaches into a bag and pulls out an LCD projector, which he sets on a table in front of the room and connects to his computer. He looks around the room and finds the stool he requested in a corner. He retrieves it and sets it on the side at the front of the room. He has found, over the years, that sitting on the stool creates a comfortable, casual feeling while allowing him to maintain a position of control while facilitating discussion.

Ross sits on the stool to test its comfort and watches Mark and Bill as they place a notebook of the slides that will be used in the session, on the table in front of each chair. Mark puts the last notebook in place and looks up at Ross. "Well, Ross, here we go again," he says. "Are you ready for another improvement journey with Global Products?"

Ross chuckles. "This should be a walk in the park, a 'piece of cake,' compared to the first time through," he says, partially in jest. "At least we're not starting from scratch this time. Each of the divisions already has some sort of S&OP process in place. With some luck, we'll find a lot of the fundamentals already in place and can get to work doing the strategic side of the process. That's the fun stuff. If we find the fundamentals lacking, we'll fix them more quickly than the first time because people are already doing some sort of S&OP."

"Ross, I hope you're right, but didn't you say this was about changing the way the management team _thinks_ about the business? It has been my experience that it is not as easy as one might believe, especially with our management team," Mark replies.

Ross understands Mark's position. It is always nerve-wracking to lead a project, not knowing what dynamics might influence the team and whether they are truly committed to creating change or are just paying lip service to the project.

"I understand your point of view, Mark. My optimism comes from Jack's strong support and the fact that you are leading the effort. I expect we will move this project along quite rapidly, at least in most of the divisions. As we found when implementing Sales and Operations Planning, one or two divisions almost always are more of a challenge than the others; but I am not worried. This should be a fun project."

Chapter **3**

Common Understanding

IT IS GREETING TIME. THE other team members start to arrive, and Ross and Mark break away to welcome each person. Mark introduces Ross to the corporate team members.

He introduces Bailey Madison, the Vice President of Supply Chain Management and Mark's co-leader on the initiative, and Taylor Jackson, Vice President of Strategic Planning. Ross shakes their hands, and they exchange pleasantries.

Ross sees Janis Novak enter the room. They need no introduction. Janis was the controller at the Universal Products division and now serves as Corporate Controller. Ross and Janis are genuinely pleased to see one another. They give each the "once-over" and joke that they may have a few more gray hairs, but appear to have withstood the years quite well.

Mark interrupts their reminiscing about "old times" to introduce Nolan Justin, Director of Information Technology. Nolan shakes Ross's hand and says, "I'm not sure why I'm here."

"By the end of the day, it should be clear why we need you," Ross replies.

Mark raises his voice to get the attention of the people pouring coffee from the urns at the back of the room and helping themselves to fruit and muffins. "Okay, guys and gals, let's get started. We have a large amount of material to cover today."

Everyone finds a seat around the u-shaped table while Mark moves to the front of the room and prepares to speak. He pauses for a few moments to make sure everyone has settled into their seats. He glances around the table and wonders, for a moment, what kind of team this group will make and what they will learn along the way.

"Good morning, team," Mark says. "I am pleased that you all are here and are on time. Thank you. As you know, I have asked Ross Peterson of Effective Management to help coach and guide us through this very important initiative. Each of you has been individually selected by Jack Baxter and me for your knowledge of Sales and Operations Planning, your experience in Global Products and Services, and your ability to influence the organization."

Mark explained that the team will serve as the core steering committee for this initiative. Members may be added periodically, as necessary, but Mark expects each team member to hold themselves accountable for successfully implementing what Mark has named GPS – IBP, Global Products and Services Integrated Business Planning.

"I have talked with each of you individually and shared that it is time to kick up our Sales and Operations Planning processes into a higher gear," Mark says.

"Based upon performance of companies across a broad range of industry, Jack and I agree that there is a considerable opportunity for our divisions to operate more effectively and to grow both the top and bottom lines. I will leave that discussion to Ross as he brings us up to date on the evolution of Sales and Operations Planning. Before I hand it over to Ross, are there any questions?"

Bailey Madison, a tall, blond-haired woman with an air of confidence, raises her hand. "Mark, is everyone here clear on the two separate but related initiatives underway? And are our two roles clear to everyone?" Mark nods in Bailey's direction. "Thanks, Bailey. I definitely should have provided more clarity on those issues." He explains to the group that the two initiatives are closely related. Do both well, and integrate both, and the company will maximize the performance improvements. He also states the expectation that one of the steering team's roles is to make sure the two initiatives end up as one integrated Global Products solution.

"The Integrated Business Planning project is an aggregate planning process aimed at integrating Strategic Management into the organization," Mark explains. "In order for decisions made in that process to be executed, the Integrated Business Planning process must be connected to the detailed planning and control processes of Global Products, specifically in the supply chain. Bailey is heading up the detailed planning and control and supply chain optimization processes. I am heading up the aggregate planning process. The two of us will be working together to make sure the aggregate and detailed processes connect."

Mark turns to Bailey. "Did I leave anything out?"

"You explained it quite well, Mark. I just wanted to reinforce the objective that both processes must connect. One of the key findings of recent research is that _improved connection to execution_ is a priority of companies operating with Sales and Operations Planning."

Ross decides that Bailey's comments create a perfect segue to his presentation. He steps forward. "Bailey is correct. You will hear me talk about something called the "Diamond," which is the name of a model some of our coaches use for connecting the decisions made in the leadership management process to execution."

Mark interrupts. "Are there any other questions before I turn this session over to Ross?" The room is quiet. "If not," Mark says, "Ross, take it away!"

Ross nodded to Mark and, in a big voice, says, "Good Morning! And welcome to this session on the transition of Sales and Operations Planning to Integrated Business Planning. It is truly a pleasure to be working with Global Products and Services once again. As you all know, I was blessed with the opportunity to help Mark and Jack implement S&OP some years ago. With a small team from Effective Management supporting Mark and his team, S&OP was successfully implemented in all divisions. The primary measure of success was improved business results. And as you know, the company has been enjoying those benefits ever since."

Ross pauses to look at Mark and Janis. "I thought that we worked together some four or five years ago. But in preparing for this session, I am amazed to see that it was nearly eight years ago that we worked to implement S&OP, starting with the Universal Products division. How time flies!"

Ross addresses the group in the same way that he usually begins to engage a team. "I know that all of you have a fundamental knowledge of Sales and Operations Planning," he says, "so my primary objectives today are to, first, get you all on the *same page* on how Sales and Operations Planning has evolved over the last eight years and, second, to gain consensus on what major areas for improvement should be set as corporate expectations and guidelines for the divisional improvement initiatives."

Ross tells the group that, unless the team decides otherwise, it is currently expected that the actual improvements and, therefore, improvement work will be done within each division. As Mark shared, the approach will be to start with a small group of leaders to gain consensus and then expand to a larger group, including the division managers and current S&OP coordinators/leaders, before beginning to make the improvements in each division.

"At least that is our assumption going into today's session," Ross says. "The real work will be done division by division. Any questions?"

The room is quiet. Ross decides to set a ground rule. "As we did in our last implementation, I am going to assume that no response means that you heard me, you understood me, and you agreed with me on the issue at hand. In short, silence means acceptance."

Janis and Mark nod knowingly. Bailey seeks clarification. "Why is silence considered acceptance?"

Ross smiles at Bailey. "I'm glad you asked. We use 'silence is acceptance' because we find when this is the ground rule, team members will more quickly point out areas of confusion or concern. This approach enables us to move forward much faster than if we simply let an issue or concern fester over time. Let me explain another principle that is closely related to 'silence is acceptance.' That is, the principle of open and honest communication, but with respect for the individual. Are we okay with these ground rules and principles?"

The team members nod their heads in agreement, but give no verbal response. "Silence is acceptance," Ross declares. "Let's move on."

Ross points the wireless remote controller at his computer and brings up a slide.

"Let's talk about the evolution of Sales and Operations Planning to Integrated Business Planning," he says. "I don't want you to think that Global Products and Services has been doing anything wrong with Sales and Operations Planning. But nothing seems to stand still any more, including Sales and Operations Planning."

Ross walks to his stool and pulls it more closely to the u-shaped table. "I have recently had the opportunity to stop and reflect on Sales and Operations Planning, its development, and evolution. My reflections took me to both the micro level, that is, at the individual company level, and at the macro or broader industry level," he says, settling down on the stool.

Ross talks uninterrupted for more than five minutes. He explains that he has learned much about Sales and Operations Planning, first as a practitioner for six years and then as an educator and coach on integrated business management processes for the past twenty-five years. He also has found recent independent research on Sales and Operations Planning quite interesting.

"Sometimes we need to stop and assess where we are going, what value we are bringing, and how we can do better. That's what caused me to reflect on Sales and Operations Planning," he says.

Ross tells the group he has come to realize that the fundamentals behind a successful Sales and Operations Planning process have not changed significantly over the years, but the emphasis and focus of the process varies considerably in different companies. What has been revealing is how the emphasis and focus of the process change as the process matures. The maturity level of S&OP processes is not determined by how many years companies have been doing Sales and Operations Planning. A great number of companies have been operating Sales and Operations Planning for years, even decades, but they still have relatively immature processes. Other companies have evolved their Sales and Operations Planning processes to a mature level rather quickly, within a year or two of operation.

"This requires some explanation," Ross says.

Before he can continue, Taylor Jackson, Vice President of Strategy, speaks up. As he speaks, Taylor sits ramrod straight in his chair and pushes his glasses further up his face. "So, Ross, or Mark, do you think that Global Products has been operating with immature or mature processes?"

Without hesitation, Mark says, "Let me respond to that, Ross. That is exactly what we will want to find out as we begin the implementation. Based upon previous conversations with Ross and with Jack, I am sure that we have a range of maturity levels."

Taylor thinks about Mark's response for a moment, but is not ready to move on. "How do we know what is mature and what is immature?"

"You're asking great questions, Taylor," Ross says. "Thank you. We're getting at the heart of why we are having this session today. First, let me say that I will be providing a *documented set of criteria* on what a mature process should look like, at both a high level and at a detailed level. We will spend some time on the high level today. The detailed level will be more important at the individual business division level. We will also discuss the first key implementation task for each division. That is what we call a diagnostic."

Bailey Madison, Vice President of Supply Chain, interrupts and turns toward Mark. "Let me make sure I understand correctly. Will we leave here today with a consensus on a high level, or executive view, of what Sales and Operations Planning or, now, Integrated Business Planning should look like for Global Products and Services, Inc.?"

"That is correct. At least, that is our objective," Mark replies.

Janis Novak turns her attention from Mark to Ross and asks, "Ross, is the criteria that you referred to, the Oliver Wight Class A Checklist we used in the implementation eight years ago?"

"That's right, Janis," Ross replies. "But you may recall our saying that Oliver Wight updates the criteria from time to time as industry advances its use of business processes. Oliver Wight now has a Sixth Edition checklist. There have been some significant changes in emphasis and scope. These changes are reflected in the Sixth Edition. Also, we will make sure that the criteria used to assess the S&OP processes in each division include the connection to execution. These criteria are key to ensuring that the Integrated Business Planning project and Bailey's detailed planning project connect and integrate. Eight years ago, it was a common practice to have a separate initiative or phase to connect to execution. Essentially, it was left to each division to do their own connection to execution. Some divisions apparently did it well; some, maybe not so well. Understanding the level of effectiveness in each division will be part of what is reviewed in the diagnostic."

Ross pauses and scans each member of the team. "Are we OK to continue?" he asks. "Silence is acceptance."

Ross advances the next visual on the screen (Figure 3). It is the standard Sales and Operations Planning process model visual that Effective Management, Inc. has used for a number of years. The model depicts the aggregate planning process that culminates in a Management Business Review conducted by the senior leadership team. The model is elliptical to show the process is conducted every month. It is the same model that Global Products used in its Sales and Operations Planning implementation eight years ago. It is the same model that Jack was surprised had changed so little over the years.

The group nods their heads at the model. They are familiar with it. Every division of Global Products had used it to implement Sales and Operations Planning.

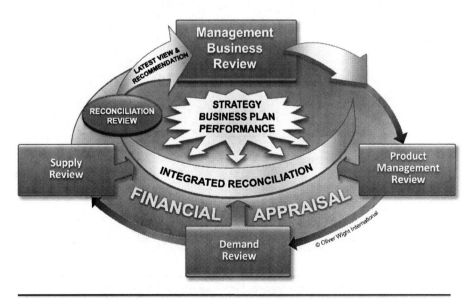

Figure 3　Sales and Operations Planning Model for Aligning Company Plans Every Month
(Copyright Oliver Wight International. Reproduced with permission.)

"To one degree or another, every division is still using this monthly process today to manage their business," Ross says. "I will share a few observations about this model and seek consensus so that we can move forward."

Ross looks at the group, studying their faces for readiness to move on. He sees that Taylor Jackson appears uncomfortable, but hesitates to speak.

"Do you have a question, Taylor?" Ross asks.

"That isn't the only model, is it?" Taylor replies. "I recall another model that is broader and shows that this S&OP process model is part of a more comprehensive integrated model."

Ross smiles at Taylor. "You're absolutely correct. Let me find it."

Ross uses the remote to scroll through several slides until he finds the model that Taylor recalls. "Here it is," he says. "You can see the Sales and Operations Planning process model at the top, which culminates in the senior leadership team's monthly Management Business Review. What this Integrated Management Process model depicts are the connections to execution."

Ross uses the laser pointer to focus on the process boxes under the Supply, Demand, and Product Management Reviews. (See Figure 4.) "As you can see," Ross says, "the Sales and Operations Planning process sits on top of the day-to-day, week-to-week planning and control processes in each of the functional areas."

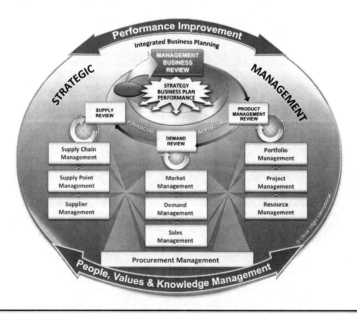

Figure 4 Integrated Business Planning Model That Connects Sales and Operations Planning To Detailed Execution (Copyright Oliver Wight International. Reproduced with permission.)

Bailey raises her hand and says, "Mark and I discussed roles for this project. In this model, Mark is the leader of the S&OP process at the top, and I am tasked with leading the detailed daily, weekly, and continuous processes below it."

"As you can see, they all need to work together," Mark says.

Nolan Justin, the Director of Information Technology, speaks for the first time. "So why are we separating this into two project activities?"

"I can answer the question in one word, *scope*," Ross says. "But I need to explain the answer in some detail using a broader context."

Ross explains that companies with an aggregate planning process (Sales and Operations Planning) at the leadership level perform better than those that don't. Research studies and Effective Management, Inc.'s own experience bear out this statement. Companies that operate with integrated detailed planning and control processes achieve significant operational performance improvements. Research studies have validated these improvements. Companies have also proven that integrating their planning and fulfillment processes with trading partners in the supply chain not only improves performance but, also, can be leveraged for a competitive advantage. To do so, these processes must operate at "best practices" levels.

"The job of implementing and operating aggregate planning at the leadership level and detailed planning and control processes, including Supply Chain Collaboration, is just too much for one project," Ross says.

"Here's where you come in, Nolan," Ross says, turning to face the Director of Information Technology. "From years of experience, we know that there is a tremendous amount of work to implement detailed planning and control processes in a company. Often this effort requires improving or changing the software tools a company uses in operations and finance."

Now Ross turns his attention to the entire group. "It's not just about addressing software tools that support detailed planning and control processes. What's even more important is focusing on the behaviors needed to support integration of the detailed planning and control processes and then operating the processes to best practice levels. I don't mean to under-value the role of information technology. Behavior change is not easy, however, and can be the most difficult to achieve."

Ross pauses and looks at each member of the team. "What I am saying is that it is a large undertaking to implement or improve detailed planning and control processes, and make sure that they are integrated with Sales and Operations Planning as well as with your trading partners, both customers and suppliers. It involves process design or redesign, tool configuration or reconfiguration, and development of the behaviors and competencies to operate the processes effectively. Depending on the size and complexity of the business, it can take 12 to 24 months to accomplish."

"In contrast," Ross explains, "Sales and Operations Planning and Integrated Business Planning are smaller in scale, compared to implementing a detailed integrated planning and control process. As a result, companies achieve improved business performance in only a few months, provided that the process is properly implemented. Behavior change is paramount with Sales and Operations Planning and Integrated Business Planning. What drives behavior change is the leadership of the company demonstrating, through its actions, that the company will be run with the integrated management process, which is different than the 'old way' of managing the company."

Ross sits down on the stool. His explanation has been long, and he wants to make sure the group understands the key points he made. It is time to summarize.

"Effective Management recommends that Sales and Operations Planning, or Integrated Business Planning, be implemented as soon and as quickly as possible. Implementing S&OP or IBP is much smaller in scale and takes less time, compared to implementing detailed planning and control."

He continues to explain that results from an S&OP or IBP process can be achieved in as little as a few months after starting. Development and implementation of detailed planning and control is also recommended. The implementation of detailed planning and control should occur in parallel with an S&OP or IBP implementation, if practical, given resource constraints. After detailed planning and control is implemented, companies then should focus on Supply Chain Collaboration.

"It is important to get your own house in order," Ross says, "before trying to integrate with your customers. You get your own house in order by implementing Sales and Operations Planning, or Integrated Business Planning, and detailed planning and control, and operating these processes to best practice standards."

Nolan, who started the discussion by asking why the two initiatives are separated, is not quite comfortable yet. "If you have resources to do only one of these two initiatives," he asks, "which initiative do you recommend doing?"

"We will make a recommendation after the diagnostic," Ross replies. "It depends on what we learn about the state of the current processes and the current business issues and opportunities."

Ross tells the group that, in most cases, Sales and Operations Planning, or Integrated Business Planning, should be implemented first, followed as quickly as practical by detailed planning and control. If resources are limited, a common approach is to implement Sales and Operations Planning, or Integrated Business Planning, and to connect the process to Master Supply Planning and Scheduling. Once that is accomplished, then focus on implementing the other elements of detailed planning and control.

"This approach is what I earlier referred to as the 'Diamond.' Nolan, with your permission, I will move on. I believe we'll develop greater clarity on priorities as we go through the day."

Nolan nods his head in agreement. Ross, however, wants to make sure Bailey is comfortable with what has been discussed and explained. As the leader of detailed planning and control and Supply Chain Optimization, Ross wants to make sure he hasn't caused her any problems.

"Bailey, are you OK with pressing on?" Ross asks. "Have I said anything that you challenge, have issue with, or wish to clarify?"

Bailey appreciates Ross's sensitivity and gives him a smile. "I am fine with all you said. Let's move on," she replies.

Chapter 4

Stuck

ROSS DECIDES TO PICK UP the pace by shifting the focus to the differences between Sales and Operations Planning and Integrated Business Planning. "Have you noticed how I've been saying Sales and Operations Planning or Integrated Business Planning? They are not really interchangeable terms. There are differences between the two processes," Ross says.

He tells the group that research studies have shown that Sales and Operations Planning, *as it is currently practiced* by many companies, is *not* what leaders and innovators of this practice call S&OP. In many, if not most, companies, the term Sales and Operations Planning describes a middle management process with a short-term focus. The process usually involves demand, supply, and inventory management at the detailed level.

The true intent of Sales and Operations Planning was an executive management process that involved aggregate planning over an intermediate and long-term planning horizon. It was never intended to only be a middle management process to balance demand, supply, and inventory over a short-term planning horizon.

Instead of arguing over the proper use of the label, "Sales and Operations Planning," people in industry, including Effective Management, Inc., decided it was time to use another label. This new label describes an executive management process involving aggregate planning that is segmented (product families, sectors, channels, and/or territories). An intermediate to long-term planning horizon is used. A number of companies were beginning to call this process Integrated Business Planning. They believe this term more accurately describes a Sales and Operations Planning process that operates to best practice standards.

In retrospect, the label Integrated Business Planning more accurately depicts the process. The process has evolved to being more than just connecting sales and operations. Today's best practice process involves the integration and alignment of the demand management, product management, supply management, financial management, strategic management, and business administration functions. As companies use the process as a strategic management process, the emphasis moves from what many call Sales and Operations Planning toward product and portfolio management. This assumes a level of maturity in the traditional demand and supply management processes.

Some companies that are operating Sales and Operations Planning at best practice levels question why people make a big deal over the name. They have a mature management process that integrates the product and portfolio management, demand management, supply management, financial management, strategic management, and business administration functions. The process is disciplined, regular, and routine in keeping all of the business plans aligned and synchronized, even in the midst of major economic, market, customer, competitive, or internally initiated changes. So, they may not care what people in industry call the process.

Ross advances the PowerPoint presentation to the following slide. "Let me share with you how one of our clients has attempted to capture the essence of the process on a single visual. Also, please take a look at the following more comprehensive maturity chart from Oliver Wight," he says.

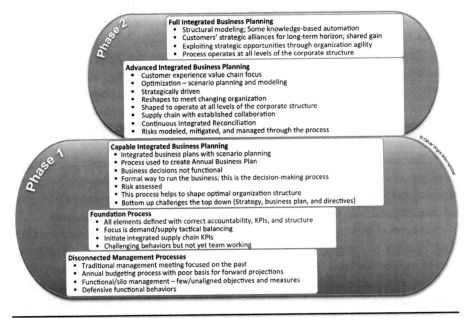

Figure 5   Process Attributes as Sales and Operations Planning Matures Into Integrated Business Planning
(Copyright Oliver Wight International. Reproduced with permission.)

Janis Novak, the Corporate Controller, reads the slide carefully. She finds herself nodding in agreement but is puzzled why Ross is emphasizing that Sales and Operations Planning is different from Integrated Business Planning. She came to respect and enjoy Ross's mentoring of her eight years ago. He won't interpret her question as a disruption.

"Ross, it seems to me this is what we set out to do in our Global Products S&OP initiative eight years ago," she says. "I think you're trying to point out a difference to us, but I don't know that I understand completely. Here's my confusion. I've had some earlier conversations with Jack. And I've been listening to your comments about how companies call processes Sales and Operations Planning that aren't really S&OP as originally conceived. It seems the primary issues center around making sure finance is integrated into the process, that new product development and product rationalization are integrated into the process, and that strategic initiatives are also part of process. Am I correct?"

Ross smiles, recalling how bright Janis is and how she never hesitates to ask for clarity. "Well stated, Janis," Ross says. "You are correct, but there is a key difference. It's what I like to call 'the essence of the business.' Many companies seem to behave as if Sales and Operations Planning is something additional that they do while they also run the business. Their attitude is that Sales and Operations Planning is something they *have* to do to make sure the supply chain is a positive contributor to the business rather than a problem."

Ross sees recognition in some people's faces, as if a light bulb has brightened. Others look confused. He needs to explain what he means by the _essence of the business_. He tells the group that companies need to use the process to discuss the key elements for business success; these discussions should not be excluded from the process.

"If client success and customer intimacy are key to the success of the business, then they should be discussed within the context of the Sales and Operations Planning/Integrated Business Planning process. If operational excellence is really the essence of the business, then it should be discussed within the context of the process. If product leadership and innovation are key to the success of the business, then they should be discussed in the context of Sales and Operations Planning," he explains.

Now the group is stirring in their chairs. Hands are raised. Ross points to Mark.

"If I understand what you are trying to tell us, there should be one primary integrated management process used by leadership and management to run the business. S&OP or IBP is not something extra we do; it is what we do to manage the business, from a business perspective, not just a supply chain perspective."

"You're correct, Mark," Ross says. "When the subject is management of the business, there should be one integrated business management process. There will be sub-processes to manage sales, marketing, product development, supply chain, accounting, human resources, etc. But there must be one integrated process where the entire picture of the business is visible to the leadership and management team."

Jack points to Taylor Jackson, the Vice President of Strategic Planning, who has been waiting patiently with his hand in the air. "Ross and Mark, if I understand you correctly, from a strategic planning perspective, I will still have a set of activities that I execute to provide the best information and innovation to the development of strategy. We will still have a strategic planning session periodically, probably at least once a year. But when it comes to communication and execution, the strategies that are developed need to be visible and integrated into the IBP or S&OP process, or whatever we decide to call it. That way, on a regular basis to the monthly S&OP cadence, we can track the effectiveness in executing the strategies and track the effectiveness of the strategies themselves."

Ross nods and smiles. He is pleased. The team is starting to understand the concept of Integrated Business Planning.

"You're right, Taylor. The strategies, the strategic initiatives, the results of the strategic initiatives, and the anticipated results should be visible on a 'continuous' basis. The best current view of performance to strategy and strategic goals is a natural part of the Integrated Business Planning process. And yes, I used the IBP label because this strategic focus and intent is in support of the *essence of the business*. Sales and Operations Planning, as practiced by many companies, does not come close to this type of process that supports the essence of the business."

The group is quiet as each team member absorbs Ross's comments. Ross gets up from the stool and walks toward the group, clicking the remote as he does so to advance to the next slide.

"Are we okay to continue?" he asks. "Silence is acceptance."

The group looks closely at the next visual. (See Figure 6.)

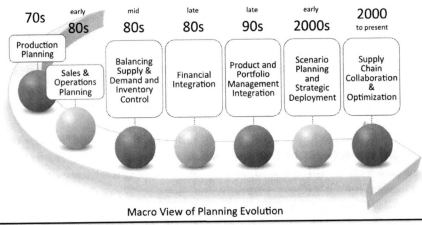

Macro View of Planning Evolution

Figure 6   Evolution of Planning (Copyright Oliver Wight International. Reproduced with permission.)

Mark explains that the slide can help to visualize some of what the group has been learning about and discussing. Many companies use the Sales and Operations Planning process to balance supply, demand, and manage inventory, but do not use it to manage the essence of the business. The management of the business is handled in some other way. For other companies, they have continued to mature and evolve the process and now use it to manage the business. This chart (Figure 6) graphs the evolution of planning. Some companies are still in the Production Planning and Sales and Operations Planning stages of evolution. Many companies have transcended to incorporating financial integration, product and portfolio management, scenario planning and strategic deployment, and supply chain collaboration and optimization.

Janis speaks up. "Ross, during our original implementation of Sales and Operations Planning, I recall you stressed the fact that implementations go through four stages. If what you have said is true, as this visual shows, doesn't this suggest that some companies stop evolving the process in the earlier stages?"

Ross laughs and claps his hands together in appreciation. "Janis, I am impressed. You remembered the four stages, eight years after being introduced to them! And you are correct in your assessment."

He turns his attention to the rest of the team, clicking the remote repeatedly until he finds the proper slide. (See Figure 7.)

"For those of you who may not have the same recollection, here's what Janis is talking about. An implementation of S&OP or IBP goes through four stages shown on this visual."

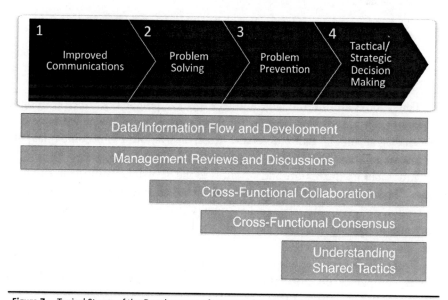

Figure 7 Typical Stages of the Development of Integrated Business Planning
(Copyright Oliver Wight International. Reproduced with permission.)

Ross flips through the notebook while the group studies the slide. "Turn to page 21 in your notebooks," he says. "Look at the detailed explanation of each stage of maturity. Take a few moments, and we will discuss any questions or thoughts you may have." (See Figure 8.)

One by one, people look up after reading through the four stages of Sales and Operations Planning and Integrated Business Planning. Ross waits patiently, wondering who will be the first to speak.

Stage 1 – Improved Communications - The process has begun. There are regularly scheduled S&OP process reviews. The data is not yet complete or trustworthy. However, issues are surfaced and discussed. This improved communications phase usually lasts through monthly cycles 1-4.

Stage 2 – Problem Solving - The regularity of the process is established. The data has improved...more complete and more trustworthy. The data shows there are problems and/or opportunities that need to be addressed in the "now" timeframe. Decisions are made and executed. This problem-solving phase usually is between cycles 3-6.

Stage 3 – Problem Prevention - The process feels more mature, disciplined, and regular. The near-term problems have largely been addressed. The management team begins focusing further out in the planning horizon. Anticipated problems are identified; decisions are made to preclude the problems from occurring. Phase three usually occurs from cycles 5-9.

Stage 4 – Tactical & Strategic Decision Making - The process has matured. Its effectiveness in identifying and enabling the solving and preventing of problems is clearly understood. The management team begins to focus on closing the gap between the current reality and the business's strategic goals and objectives. The management agenda tends to shift from problems to opportunities. The data is the best the company has, and it is used to set the expectations for the following fiscal year. i.e. The numbers drive the annual planning process.

Note: In practice, elements of all phases occur in each cycle, but the above descriptions are a reminder that in an IBP/S&OP implementation, there is a natural progression to a fully capable process.

Figure 8 Four Stages of Implementing Integrated Business Planning/Sales and Operations Planning
(Copyright Oliver Wight International. Reproduced with permission.)

Bailey looks around the table and sees that everyone has finished reading the descriptions. "It sounds like the industry, from a macro view, has stalled somewhere between Stage 2 and 3," Bailey observes. "Ross, do you know why companies fail to fully mature to Stage 4?"

Ross picks up the remote and advances to the next slide. Pointing to the visual, he says, "Here's what I think has happened. I read an interesting book recently by Seth Godin. Seth is an interesting fellow who writes and speaks about management theory and marketing concepts. He wrote the best-selling book, *Linchpin*. He also wrote the book, *the dip*."

Ross tells the team about one of the principles in *the dip* that may shed light on why companies do not fully mature their Sales and Operations Planning processes. Seth Godin writes that as people strive to become accomplished at some endeavor, they put forth focused time and effort, and they achieve visible, measureable results.

Ross uses his laser pointer to circle the red light on the middle of the visual where the words, *the dip*, are printed. (See Figure 9.) He explains that, after the initial time and effort to launch an endeavor, people come to a point where more effort and energy is required to truly achieve a high degree of performance.

"Here's the point that Seth Godin makes; it applies to most business endeavors, too," Ross says.

He pauses, then raises his voice to say, "Most people don't put forth the necessary effort to achieve the full results of an endeavor."

Figure 9 Seth Godin's Concept in *the dip* Applies to Sales and Operations Planning or Integrated Business Planning (Copyright Oliver Wight International. Reproduced with permission.)

Ross stops to gauge the reaction of the group. He can see that they are studying the visual and thinking about what he has said. He decides to use his personal life to illustrate the point.

"Let me speak to *the dip* from a personal perspective," he says. "I could draw multiple curves for multiple personal efforts. The curves would look just like the curve in this visual. All of my efforts ended in my getting stuck in 'the dip.' I have a curve for my golf game, my guitar playing, my fly fishing, my tennis game."

The team starts to giggle. "I see you get the picture," Ross says to more laughter.

Janis interrupts the laughter. "If this principle applies to companies as you say, I want to make an observation," she says. "We realized considerable benefits from implementing S&OP through Stages 1 and 2. It was relatively easy to justify that effort in financial terms. There were lower costs, improved customer service resulting in increased sales, and lower working capital. It may be a natural response to stop at Stage 2. We can say we implemented the process, and look at the all the benefits we received."

Janis pauses to gauge the response of the group. Mark uses the time to offer his own thought.

"I read *the dip*, too," he says. "There may be an even more important principle in the book. That is, there are *huge* rewards for being the *best,* for striving for and achieving excellence in performance. Look at the visual. See the increase in results after the dip."

"You're both right," Ross says. "This is also what independent research shows. Those companies that do Sales and Operations Planning, or Integrated Business Planning will *significantly* outperform other companies, not just by a little bit but significantly!"

He advances to the next slide, and then another, letting the group study the results documented by independent research firms. (See Figure 10.)

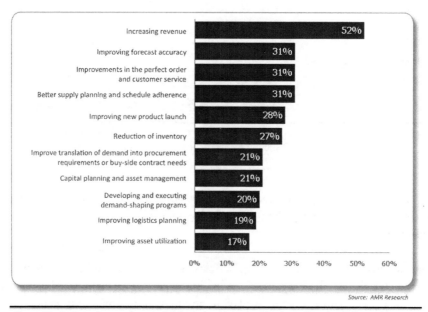

Source: AMR Research

Figure 10 Business Improvements Attributed to Integrated Business Planning/Sales and Operations Planning (Copyright Oliver Wight International. Reproduced with permission.)

When eyes focus back on Ross, he proceeds with his explanation. "I will tell you that Effective Management has clients that refuse to let us talk about the level of improvements and financial results achieved from their Sales and Operations Planning and Integrated Business Planning efforts because they see it as a huge competitive advantage. They don't care if their competitors do Sales and Operations Planning in a mediocre manner. *By continuing to evolve the process to Integrated Business Planning and operating the process well, they are outperforming their competitors hands down.*"

Bailey interrupts. Ross is not worried. To the contrary, he can see that the group is really beginning to understand, and their enthusiasm is building.

"From a supply chain management perspective," Bailey observes, "Sales and Operations Planning is getting a lot of attention because of improved supply organization performance. What I am learning from this discussion is that there are significantly *more* benefits that can be attained if a company embraces Integrated Business Planning as the way to run the business, managing the *essence of the business,* as you put it."

"Great timing, Bailey," Ross says as he clicks the remote to advance to the next slide. (See Figure 11.)

Ross explains that the innovation adoption model shown on the slide was first introduced by Everett Rogers in the early 1960s.[1] In essence, the model depicts the acceptance of innovative ideas, products, or technology that is introduced into the market. It starts with innovators, then early adopters, followed by the early majority, the late majority, and finally the laggards. Some ideas and innovations take a long time to gain acceptance and cross the chasm to the early and late majority phase. Many, or most, ideas don't make it at all.

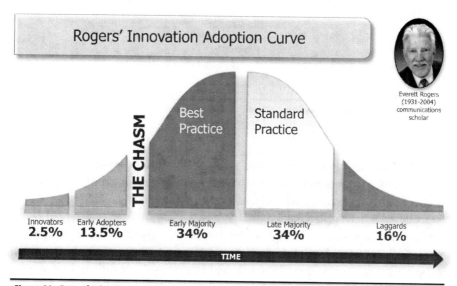

Figure 11 Rate of Adoption (Copyright Oliver Wight International. Reproduced with permission.)

"I believe that Sales and Operations Planning has taken a couple of decades to get across the chasm," Ross says. "Moreover, the S&OP process that is now heading toward becoming standard in the industry is not fully Integrated Business Planning.

[1] Rogers, Everett, *Diffusion of Innovations,* Free Press, 1962.

Rather, it is Sales and Operations Planning in Stages 1 and 2 of maturity, possibly with a few of the attributes of Stage 3."

Ross advances to the next slide, which shows the steps in the evolution of integrated planning and management. (See Figure 12.) He does not say a word. He lets the group scrutinize the slide and enjoys watching heads nod and eyes sparkle as the group realizes the point that is being made.

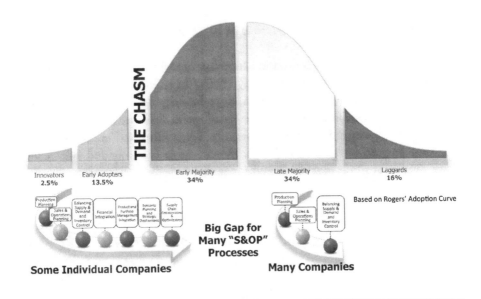

Figure 12 Today's Rate of Adoption – Sales and Operations Planning and Integrated Business Planning
(Copyright Oliver Wight International. Reproduced with permission.)

Mark pushes his chair back and walks to the screen, pointing at the visual. "Ross, I think I understand what you have been telling us this morning. Though a number of the innovators and early adopters implemented all four stages of what historically has been called Sales and Operations Planning, the majority of companies only implemented it through Stages 1 and 2 or Stages 1, 2, and 3. But these companies have not achieved the full benefits that come from using the process as a strategic management process. To mature to Stage 4 requires a different set of behaviors, working on opportunities rather than focusing only on solving problems."

"You're correct," Ross says. "At least, that has been my personal observations and is what the most current research shows. I believe, for Global Products, the opportunity is to fine tune Stages 1 through 3 and then to focus on Stage 4, Strategic Management."

Taylor joins Mark at the screen. He demonstrates his strategic perspective and his excitement about what is being discussed.

"So the adoption curve also relates to *the dip* discussion," he says. "Companies get results in Stages 1, 2, and 3. But if there isn't continued attention to the process and the focus does not evolve from operational problem solving and prevention to Strategic Management, they get *stuck* in the dip. Additional work is required to achieve proactive Strategic Management and ensure that strategic goals are achieved. My interpretation, Ross, is that IBP, or S&OP, is a real boon to strategists, who always struggle to get strategies executed. This is the process to help ensure that strategies get executed!"

"Let's explore your point a bit further, Taylor," Ross says. He asks the team to pull out a handout from their reference material in their notebooks entitled, *Strategic Planning: An Executive's Aid For Strategic Thinking, Development, and Deployment,* by George Palmatier.[2]

"Please read page 5," Ross instructs. As everyone reads page 5 of the article, Ross peruses it again himself. He has found this particular white paper to be very helpful in getting clients into a strategic *thinking* mode. He likes that the white paper is easy to read and right on point.

The white paper contains quotes from respected business management thought leaders. The first quote is from Peter Drucker, who said:

The best plan is *only* a plan; that is, good intentions, unless it *degenerates into work.*[3]

The second quote is from Robert S. Kaplan and David P. Norton on the execution of strategy:

A study of 275 portfolio managers reported that the ability to execute strategy was more important than the quality of the strategy itself...In the early 1980s, a survey of management consultants reported that fewer than 10 percent of effectively developed strategies were successfully implemented. More recently, a 1999 *Fortune* cover story of prominent CEO failures concluded that the emphasis placed on strategy and vision created a mistaken belief that the right strategy was all that was needed to succeed. In the majority of cases — we estimate 70% — the real problem isn't bad strategy but...bad execution...With the rapid changes in technology, competition and regulations, the formulation and implementation of strategy must become a continual participative process. [4]

Ross reads the third quote, which he feels illustrated well the need for a focus on execution. It was written by Larry Bossidy and Ram Charan:

[2] Palmatier, George, *Strategic Planning: An Executive's Aid For Strategic Thinking, Development, And Deployment; www.oliverwight.com.*
[3] Drucker, Peter, *The Practice of Management*, Collins, 1963.
[4] Kaplan, Robert S.; Norton, David P.; *The Strategy Focused Organization: How Balanced Scorecard Companies Thrive in the New Business Environment,* Harvard Business Press, 2000.

Execution will help you, as a business leader, to choose a more robust strategy. In fact, you can't craft a worthwhile strategy if you don't at the same time make sure your organization has or can get what's required to execute it, including the right resources and the right people. Leaders in an execution culture design strategies that are more road maps than rigid paths enshrined in fat planning books. That way they can respond quickly when the unexpected happens. Their strategies are designed to be executed.[5]

Seeing that the team members have finished reading page 5 in the white paper, Ross says, "The real issue I want you to think about is that the greatest strategy, if not executed, is worth very little. A poor strategy executed well will deliver some level of results."

He explains that a regular and routine strategic management process (also known as Integrated Business Planning) will identify problems with a poor strategy quickly, which enables making quick adjustments. The monthly framework and cadence established in Sales and Operations Planning is the perfect regular and routine process to monitor and manage strategy.

"The *primary* difference between S&OP and IBP is the strategic management element of the process," Ross emphasizes. "And, this places an increased emphasis on the first step of the process, Product and Portfolio Management."

Ross glances at the clock in the back of the room. It's time for a break. "Is everyone okay?" he asks. "If there are no immediate questions, let's take a break. We will start up again promptly in fifteen minutes."

---

[5] Bossidy, Larry; Charan, Ram; *Execution: The Discipline of Getting Things Done,* Crown Business 2002, page 7.

CHAPTER 5

The Difference Between Sales and Operations Planning and Integrated Business Planning

MARK MOTIONS ROSS TO JOIN him outside. Mark is worried about time constraints. "I know there is much more that we could discuss about the evolution of Sales and Operations Planning and the principles of Integrated Business Planning," Mark says. "But I'm worried whether we are leaving enough time to address the connection to execution. I also want to make sure we leave time to talk about the implementation plans."

Ross explains that he has considered the approach for the discussion on the connection to execution, and there will be ample time for that discussion. The discussion will be from an executive-level perspective. The connection to execution should be addressed in detail at the division level.

"We need to be sure to provide enough information so that the team agrees that connection to execution is necessary," Ross says. "This is also a key integration point for you and Bailey, since she will be leading the detailed execution side of this work. The next section of the education summarizes the differences between Sales and Operations Planning and Integrated Business Planning. After that, we will discuss connection to execution. We should have plenty of time at the end of the day to talk about implementation."

Mark feels more comfortable and thanks Ross for the explanation. They go separate ways to quickly check their emails and phone messages for anything that is urgent. Neither of them will respond to non-urgent messages. Today's session takes priority over other routine, daily issues.

Ross returns to the meeting room and is pleased to see that the team members have returned as well and are chatting together amiably. Ross announces that the session will start again in one minute. He wants to keep control of the time for breaks. Undisciplined breaks are an easy way to waste precious time in a one-day session.

Janis Novak is the last to take her seat. As she gets comfortable, Ross thanks everyone for their promptness. He lets the team know the plan for the rest of the day, mindful of Mark's concerns. He explains the same plan that he shared with Mark. He also wants to make sure that Mark and Bailey don't have anything more to add to the morning discussion about the evolution of Sales and Operations Planning.

"Mark and Bailey, do either of you have any comments, questions, or issues you want to discuss before we address the principal differences between Sales and Operations Planning and Integrated Business Planning?" Both shake their heads 'no' and motion to move forward with the presentation.

Ross sits on the stool to address the whole team. He tells them that he will highlight the differences between S&OP and IBP, but before doing so, he wants to emphasize one key point. Even those companies that are only in Stage 1 and 2 of maturity with Sales and Operations Planning achieve real, tangible benefits from the process. In many cases, those benefits are significant.

Encouraging companies to transition to Integrated Business Planning should not be interpreted as criticism of the work already accomplished in implementing and operating Sales and Operations Planning. A focus on the maturity level of the Sales and Operations Planning process is meant to emphasize that there is more to be gained – significantly more, in fact – from the effort.

"Most companies don't realize that there's more to be gained by operating the process with a focus on Integrated Business Planning rather than solely on Sales and Operations Planning. We are frequently asked, "What is the difference between Sales and Operations Planning and Integrated Business Planning?" Ross says. He advances the PowerPoint presentation to the next chart, which summarizes the differences (Figure 13).

1. More Robust Financial Integration
2. Inclusion of Strategic Plans, Initiatives, and Activities
3. More Robust Product and Portfolio Review
4. Improved Simulation, Modeling, and Scenarios
5. Improved Management of Risks and Opportunities
6. Gap Identification, Improved Decision Making
7. Easy, Effective Translation – Aggregate and Detail
8. Improved Trust Across the Entire Management Team

Figure 13 Gains Attributed to Integrated Business Planning
(Copyright Oliver Wight International. Reproduced with permission.)

"Take a minute or two to study these differences. Then, we will discuss your thoughts and questions," Ross says. "If you need additional information, a more detailed comparison is provided in the back of your notebooks." (See Appendix.)

As the group studies the slide, Ross adds, "One more key difference in the IBP process is the leadership role for Integrated Reconciliation. For an increasing number of companies, it has become a critical, full-time activity, particularly in large companies and companies with multiple divisions or businesses."

Janis is the first to raise her hand. She asks a question that a controller would be expected to ask. "So what do you mean by better financial integration?"

Ross explains that financial integration means deriving financial projections and other financial data and information from the operational plans and numbers. "Some people call this one set of numbers," Ross explains.

Ross makes several other key points relating to the financial integration:

- The measuring and reporting of actual financial performance, from a historical perspective, is fairly straightforward.
- The challenge is structuring the financial information so that it supports each element of the Integrated Business Planning process.
- The financial information needs to be in the language of how the leadership team chooses to manage the business. Orienting financial information around what the entire leadership team needs collectively sometimes requires a shift in approach by the financial group in a company.
- The forward-looking financial projections are derived directly from product portfolio changes, demand, supply, and capital plans, which are routinely updated.
- The projected income statement, cash flow, and balance sheet should be reviewed monthly as part of the Integrated Business Planning process. The information contained in the income statement, cash flow, and balance sheet should be presented in monthly time periods, not just quarterly.
- The concept of rolling planning processes and extended planning horizons should be beginning to take shape.

"I think we're already doing what you are saying," Janis says. "At least, most of the divisions are doing so and, definitely, we're doing these things at the corporate level."

"I expect this is true," Ross replies. "It was part of the original Sales and Operations Planning implementation. But we believe some divisions are integrating the financial information less well than others. We'll confirm that when we conduct the diagnostics."

Bailey's hand shoots up. "How do you know how well the financial integration is being done? Isn't it about behaviors, too? It seems to me that in some divisions the financial organization second-guesses the forecast and develops their own numbers."

"Let me answer Bailey's question," Mark says. "If what you say is true, Bailey, we may have a process problem, behavior issue, or both. It indicates that one or more of the functional leaders is not living up to their part of the process."

"I'd like to provide a perspective," Ross responds. He points out that the finance organization has a fiduciary responsibility to the corporation. If the finance group can't trust the numbers generated from the process, they have a responsibility to say so in a highly transparent manner. The Integrated Business Planning team should report the key operational performance indicators or measures each month against the commitment to the corporation ("Annual Budget" or "Annual Commitment") and to the latest rolling IBP plan. Doing so ensures that everyone on the leadership and management team can see how each area of the company is performing.

"Each executive is expected to speak to his or her variances," Ross says. "This approach is used to build accountability, and accountability is how you improve performance and build trust."

Janis raises another question. She recalls something Ross taught them during the original Sales and Operations Planning implementation: A key indicator of the quality of the projected financials and operational numbers was whether the output of the Sales and Operations Planning could be used directly to develop next year's annual commitment.

"Is that still your view?" Janis asks.

"Absolutely," Ross responds with a smile. "I just love it when a client remembers what we taught them eight years ago."

Taylor stands, places his hands on his hips, and stretches his back. An old athletic injury is acting up. In mid-stretch, he comments, "The second item on the list is about integrating strategy. This is what we discussed before, right?"

Ross confirms Taylor's observation, remarking that some process mechanics are needed to update and report the status of the strategic initiatives. Ross emphasized that Integrated Business Planning, or Sales and Operations Planning, does not replace the need to develop strategies in support of strategic goals. Nor does it replace strategic deployment of major strategic initiatives. Development and deployment of strategy is a separate process, just like product development is a separate process.

"Once the strategy is developed, articulated, communicated, and deployed, the leadership team monitors results and progress toward achieving the strategy through each step in the process," Ross says. "If gaps or opportunities are identified, action is taken to address them."

The fourth item on the list, simulation and modeling, intrigues Nolan Justin, the Director of Information Technology. "I assume software tools are needed to support simulation and modeling, and that a more mature IBP process will require a more complete set of tools to support the process," he states.

"Excellent observation, Nolan." Ross responds.

Ross tells the group that the fourth item on the list also relates to items 5, 6 and 7. Uncertainties always exist and must be managed. This can be accomplished by developing "what-if" scenarios. The models are based on making changes to key variables, like volume, mix, price, cost, etc., so that the management and leadership teams can see the consequences of different conditions and choices, given different sets of variables. With these multiple scenarios, better decisions can be made, and contingency plans can be developed in advance of a range of realities actually occurring.

Nolan is clearly interested in the software required to support Integrated Business Planning. He obviously has been thinking about the capabilities that are required of IBP tools.

"So, is the ability to convert aggregate data to detailed data, and vice versa, key? I ask because I don't believe the leadership team will necessarily want or need information at the same level of detail as the management team," Nolan says. "The management team may need more detailed information in the individual steps of the process to more clearly model the impact of each scenario, which will help to make a more informed decision or recommendation."

"That's right, Nolan," Ross responds.

Before Ross can say anything more on the subject Nolan has raised, Bailey speaks up. She explains that in the discovery work she has done on integrated planning, a frequent complaint of Sales and Operations Planning process coordinators was that they didn't have enough time to properly analyze and synthesize the information and data. Most of their time was spent gathering the data.

"If I understand what Nolan said, we are probably going to want to review the S&OP software we currently use. We may need to supplement the current software or use different software to support Sales and Operations Planning, aka IBP. In order to accomplish simulation, modeling, and scenario planning, we are going to have to make data gathering and presentation more efficient. Otherwise, the S&OP/IBP process leads will not have the time needed to develop scenarios or analyze the impact of potential risks and opportunities. We won't improve our decision making either. Are my conclusions correct?" Bailey asks.   Janis speaks before Ross can answer Bailey's question. He sits on the stool. He is enjoying the discussion and is encouraged that the team grasps the key concepts of Integrated Business Planning and what is needed to effectively operate the process.

"The situation Bailey describes may be different in different divisions as well," Janis says. She notes that each division uses different systems and software. She suggests to the team that guidance from Corporate on the information that needs to be created for Sales and Operations Planning, or Integrated Business Planning, will be needed.

Janis surveys the team. "I may be acting selfishly, but we are going to want to see the financial projections rolled up to one corporate view as easily as possible," she says.

Ross stands up and pushes away from the stool. He walks toward to group.

"This is a good discussion, and I have no argument with anything that has been said," Ross states. "I do want to caution you, though, that this is not primarily a tools-oriented project. Tools are important and necessary, and Global Products will need to manage the tool effort. The most significant benefits from the project will come from improved integration, more forward visibility and transparency, and more strategic thinking."

Mark observes that Global Products has demonstrated that improved decision making was one of the most significant benefits from the initial Sales and Operations Planning implementation. That does not mean that better tools will not be needed, however.

"Jack and I are open to using a new set of tools, if we decide that is what is needed. We don't necessarily want to work off of multiple sets of spreadsheets," Mark says.

Ross believes it is important to reemphasize a point made earlier around developing the data and information to support Integrated Business Planning – and the time required to do so, especially if dependent upon manual tools. "With the availability of detailed information from customers and markets, the amount of data to process and manage may necessitate better tools, especially as you connect detailed execution to aggregate and vice versa," he explains.

Bill Williams, the project integration leader, has been quiet during most of the discussions. He's been thinking about the last item on the list that addresses improved trust among the management team.

"I think I understand the differences between S&OP and IBP that are listed. But isn't the last item, trust, a resultant of doing the other items well? Doesn't trust result from having greater visibility and more transparency? I'm thinking in terms of my role as project integration leader. Is there something specific, from a project management point of view, that we need to do to help facilitate the development of trust across the entire management team?"

Mark feels the need to demonstrate leadership. He pushes back his chair and walks to the front of the room to stand near Ross.

"Bill, you are absolutely correct, and that is why you are part of this team," Mark says.

Mark turns toward the entire team. He explains that trust among the management team was developed as a result of Sales and Operations Planning during the original implementation. With greater transparency and visibility of the plans, tactics, and issues of each functional area, the leadership team members gained the opportunity to understand, to question, and to challenge other members of the team. By the way, this was not a "food fight." The discussions were respectful, and the management team members came to see that different perspectives had real value. It helped in making better decisions and to fully understand the impacts and ramifications of those decisions.

"Let me emphasize one point, though," Mark says. "When the leadership team completed the Management Business Review, we had reached consensus on _one plan_ that we held ourselves accountable to deliver. We also knew that we trusted each leadership team member and management member to support that plan."

Mark scans the team members, meeting each member with his eyes. After giving the team a moment to think about what he had said, Mark turns to Ross.

"Do you have any comments on what I've recalled, Ross?" Mark asks.

Ross begins to search his computer for a specific slide. "I want to revisit a previous visual describing another client's experience," he says, pointing to the slide on the screen. (See Figure 14.) "This client attempted to capture the essence of what we just discussed on a single page."

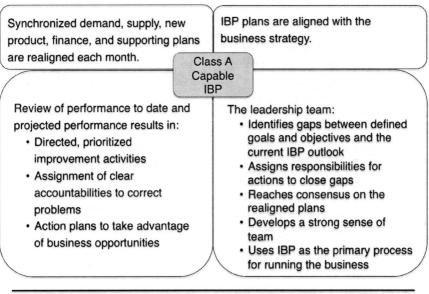

Figure 14 Attributes That Companies Cite When Operating to Class A Capable Levels
(Copyright Oliver Wight International. Reproduced with permission.)

"I concur with what Mark said about developing greater trust among the leadership team members," Ross continues. "Note that my other client used the words, 'a strong sense of team,' to describe one of the attributes of operating their Integrated Business Planning at a Class A Capable level. Trust is the foundational step in developing teamwork. I would like to review one other fundamental principle. That is, each team member commits 'to do what they say they are going to do.'"

Ross feels it is important to explain this principle in detail, even though several of the team members have heard it before during the original implementation and have abided by it during the ensuing years.

"During each monthly Integrated Business Planning cycle, we expect the metrics and key performance indicators to tell us whether we collectively and individually are doing what we said we would do. If the answer is 'No', we expect to understand why we have not executed. We also expect to take action to correct the situation. The action could be anything from changing strategy to simply performing root cause analysis and fixing the problem," Ross says.

Ross advances the PowerPoint presentation that lists Class A behaviors. (See Figure 15.) Heads nod in recognition of the visual. It was originally introduced eight years before.

"As you recall, there are several corollaries to the principle of 'do what you say you are going to do,'" Ross says.

- Do What You Say You're Going to Do
- Do Not Promise More Than You Can Deliver
- Deliver What You Promise...Or Communicate
- Open and Honest Communications
- No "Shooting the Messenger"
- Continuous Rolling Replanning vs. Annual Planning Mentality
- Managing Change
- Planning, Execution Systems, and Communications Are Synchronized
- **One Set of Integrated Numbers!**

Figure 15   Examples of Class A Behaviors
(Copyright Oliver Wight International. Reproduced with permission.)

Mark is still standing next to Ross, and he takes over. "I hope we all remember these principles from the initial implementation," Mark says. Heads continue to nod.

"We are going to break for lunch," Mark continues. "But before we do so, do we have consensus that we will continue to operate with these Class A behaviors?"

Heads nod; the team is silent. "That's our first consensus decision. After lunch, I will lead a short discussion to get consensus on a couple of more key items," Mark says.

People begin to push back their chairs. Mark looks at his watch. "Lunch is outside the room. Let's agree to be back in forty-five minutes."

Chapter 6

Consensus on the Basics

LUNCH IS PLEASANT WITH LOTS of informal chitchat about current events and life in general. The team eats their salads and sandwiches quickly and, almost as one, pushes away from the table with cell phones in hand. Time to check phone messages and emails before the session resumes.

Ross, Mark, and Bailey find themselves migrating outside together. The weather is fine, and a short walk on this warm day will be refreshing, especially after sitting indoors all morning.

They walk a little ways in quiet introspection. When they reach the curve in the exit to the hotel and turn around to go back to the meeting room, Ross asks the two project leaders, "How do you two feel we are doing so far?"

Bailey is quick to respond. "I'm comfortable, but am somewhat concerned that we have a lot more to talk about. We are trying to get a lot done in one day."

Mark gives Ross a sidelong glance. "During the break, Ross and I agreed we need to discuss connection to execution and implementation. If we accomplish that today, I will be happy."

Ross tells Bailey, "Mark and I did talk about being sure that we address connection to execution, which, of course, is key for your project. But, I cautioned him, it would be a high-level, executive discussion. More detailed discussions will be needed, but are more appropriate to conduct in each division separately."

Bailey nods in agreement, "You and I discussed that earlier as well. What's important from my perspective is that this core team understands that aggregate planning is necessary for the leadership team, but that none of our divisions makes or buys or develops products in aggregate. In order to execute, we must be planning and executing at the detailed level."

As they reach the revolving doors to the hotel, Mark nods and says, "I think we are all in sync. We're ready for the afternoon session."

Ross and Bailey find the restrooms while Mark continues toward the meeting room. His Blackberry vibrates, and Mark finds a message from Jack Baxter.

Though Jack is in Japan for business meetings, he has taken the time to send Mark a message of encouragement. He also asks Mark to let the team know he is expecting to see movement on this initiative quickly. Mark smiles to himself. So like Jack, at once, pushing and encouraging. He knows, just like the other initiatives, Jack will be a key resource when personalities or leadership issues need to be addressed.

Mark stands at the front and center of the room, waiting for everyone to reassemble. Ross joins Mark up front, and Mark tells Ross he would like to start the afternoon session with a few brief words.

"Team," Mark says, "we had a good discussion this morning. Just so you know our afternoon priorities, Bailey and I have asked Ross to move into connection of leadership decisions to execution, and then we will discuss implementation. But, before we get started with those discussions, I want to make sure we have consensus on a couple of items."

Mark scans the room. He has everyone's full attention. "Remember, silence is acceptance." Heads nod in agreement.

"First, I am looking for consensus that this project is the right thing to do," Mark says. " Does anyone have any comment or disagreement?"

Janis raises her hand. "I agree that it is the right thing to do, but we have to expect that each division will be in a different current state with the process. Some will have more work to do than others. Some will feel that they are already there."

"Isn't that why Ross said we should start with a diagnostic at each division?" Nolan asks.

Mark confirms that Nolan's statement is correct, and the diagnostics will be part of this afternoon's discussion on implementation.

Mark looks around the room to see if anyone else desires to speak. "Are there any other questions or comments? If not, then our consensus decision is that we, as a team, support this effort."

All heads nod in agreement, and Mark tackles the next consensus question. "We need to agree upon the name for this improvement initiative. These are my thoughts on the subject. The objective of this initiative is to fully implement all elements of the Integrated Business Planning process, and we will call it the Integrated Business Planning process. To do so will involve transitioning from Sales and Operations Planning to Integrated Business Planning. Therefore, the project will be communicated as a project _to transition from S&OP to IBP_."

Bailey interjects quickly, "For sure, this name covers the planning process going through all four stages of implementation to become a process for Strategic Management. But, do you mean that the name covers the project to connect the IBP plans to the detailed planning and control processes as well as execution?"

Mark's expression shows surprise at Bailey's question.

Ross decides to add his input. "Let me suggest that the scope of the Integrated Business Planning project should include the leadership planning process _and_ _connection_ to the next level of execution."

Mark explains that this next level of execution is Master Supply Planning and Scheduling (not just for the supply chain but for product development and strategic projects as well). But the project to transition from S&OP to IBP does not include the other detailed planning and control processes that receive the output of the Master Supply Planning and Scheduling processes. The connection of Master

Supply Planning and Scheduling to the other detailed planning and control processes is a different kind of work that will involve different people in each division. To lump the detailed processes into the aggregate leadership planning process of Integrated Business Planning will get too complex. Integrated Business Planning can be implemented more quickly than detailed planning and control, or what some people call Supply Chain Planning or Supply Chain Optimization.

"You don't want to unnecessarily extend the implementation time for Integrated Business Planning and miss out on the readily available benefits from the process," Ross explains. "Conversely, you want to be able to structure the detailed planning and control process (Supply Chain Planning and Optimization) properly and enable it to be implemented on its own, optimal time line."

Mark, appearing more at ease, nods his head in agreement. "I agree with Ross," he says. "So, let me restate the consensus statement. I am looking for consensus on calling the leadership management process, Integrated Business Planning. The implementation project for Integrated Business Planning will include the four stages of implementing the aggregate management process and will include connecting the Integrated Business Planning process to the next level of execution, as above. The project at the detailed level in the functional areas will be done under a different banner or name, but must integrate with the overall company Integrated Business Planning process."

Before continuing, Mark pauses and looks around the room at each team member. "I hope that we are clear on each project, including the name and scope of Integrated Business Planning. I hope we are also clear that the detailed planning and execution initiative will need to be named at some point in the future. Do we have consensus?"

Bailey, as the appointed executive leader of the detailed processes, quickly says, "I agree."

Taylor Jackson is not quite ready to move on. "Mark, my notes from this morning show that you wanted to call this effort the "GPS-IBP" project," he says. "Is this part of your request for consensus?

"No fair keeping track of what I said, Taylor," Mark replies, with a chuckle. Mark refreshes the group with what he said earlier in the day. He had been referring to Global Products and Services' Integrated Business Planning process. Condensed into three letter acronyms, it becomes GPS IBP.

"From a corporate perspective, GPS IBP is correct," Mark says. "But it would not work as a name for each division's IBP process. So, I suggest that each division call their process by the division name plus Integrated Business Planning. Anyone disagree?"

All of the team members were silent. "It is done then!" Mark says.

"GPS actually has a double meaning," Mark says to the group.

Ross knows where Mark's comments are headed and scrolls through the PowerPoint presentation. He pulls up a visual that shows a global positioning system. (See Figure 16.)

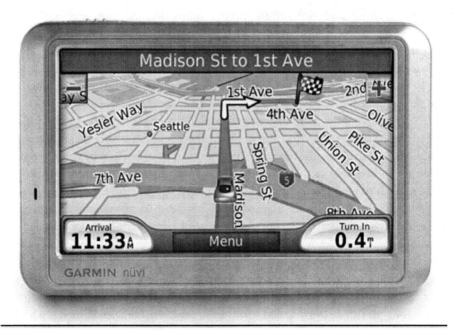

Figure 16   Integrated Business Planning Is the Global Positioning System for Businesses – Plan and Replan (Copyright Oliver Wight International. Reproduced with permission.)

Mark points to the visual and says, "In calling our process GPS IBP, I wanted to take advantage of the metaphor being used to illustrate the power of IBP. That is, a global positioning device for the business, where you can plan and replan your route to your destination."

The team members look mildly amused. Nolan, grinning, finally says, "OK, Mark, we get it. Is there anything else we need to reach consensus on?"

Mark shakes his head. "Not at the moment," he replies.

Mark returns to his seat. Ross takes center stage.

Ross explains to the group that he is going to review a high-level summary of a typical Integrated Business Planning process and what occurs during the monthly cycle of operating the process. He projects on the screen the traditional model for Sales and Operations Planning. (See Figure 17.)

Mark explains to the group the assumption is that the leadership team and management team have established a disciplined, regular, and routine monthly process to align and synchronize the business. The process is repetitive. Thus, information and decisions from each review are ultimately communicated to all those actively participating in the process.

He points at the Product Management Review box in the visual and explains that the product and service portfolio is reviewed each month for changes that occur

Figure 17 Sales and Operations Planning Model (Copyright Oliver Wight International. Reproduced with permission.)

during the month. These changes may be the addition of new products or services. The changes may be deletions of products and services. The key point is that any *significant* product or service changes are identified and communicated.

What is communicated is not just from a historical perspective – what has occurred in the past. The future perspective is most important; that is, changes that are planned and anticipated over the rolling planning horizon. As a company moves from S&OP to IBP, the underlying thought process moves from being more execution oriented to strategy oriented. The time in discussion moves more from near-term product and project management to longer-term product portfolio and market strategy.

Other information is also communicated through the Product Management Review (PMR). The project status on new products and product rationalizations needs to be updated. Decisions that take place in the ongoing product portfolio and stage and gate processes need to be visible to all participants.

Ross wraps up the description of the Product Management Review by emphasizing that, each month, it should provide the best, most current view of the company's product and service offering across the full planning horizon. This requires both short-term and long-term thinking and integration of execution and planning. Providing a consolidated set of information in the Product Management Review enables improved product portfolio management. This information makes it possible to identify the impact of the latest product and service portfolio changes on the demand plan, supply capability and other resources, and on the company's strategic and financial goals. If there are constraints, or if the latest changes impact the financial and strategic goals, the flag should be raised to communicate that decisions or direction is required. One decision may be that there is a need to revisit the strategy. The decision may be a change to the business strategy, or it may be a change to the product and service strategy, or both.

Ross pauses to look around the room. "Are there any questions on the Product Management Review?"

Taylor speaks up, "Earlier you said that in IBP, there is a greater emphasis on product portfolio management. To me, this implies fixing or improving support processes, like idea filtering, stage and gate processes, portfolio management, and project management processes and reporting, etc. Would you agree?"

Ross is pleased and, as he looks over at Mark, he sees that Mark is pleased as well. "Yes, Taylor, you are correct. The first priority of the product portfolio management step is to ensure integration with the rest of the organization. As this process step matures, and the basic support processes improve, the PMR moves more toward portfolio management.

Ross brings forward a slide showing a typical innovation funnel (Figure 18). "As companies move to IBP with greater strategic emphasis," he says, "the management of innovation and connection to strategic goals and strategies will continue to increase in importance as the process matures. As the process matures, key innovations and projects will become more visible in various information displays to the full management and leadership team. Questions?"

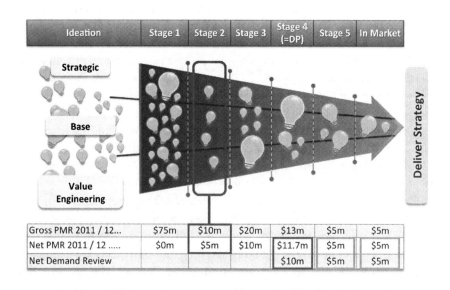

Figure 18   Visibility of the Innovation Funnel Is Key for IBP Processes

The team is quiet. Ross takes silence as permission to move forward.

"Let's take a look at the Demand Review," he says.

He explains to the group that the updated view of the product and service portfolio serves as input into the Demand Management process and the Demand Review. The Demand Review does not just focus on the performance to the demand plan to date. It also includes a review of the external business environment and the potential impact on demand. The review of the external business environment should consider, as a minimum, the economy, markets, customers, channels, and the competition.

Some key questions should be asked and answered during the Demand Review. These questions include:

- Are we selling what we said we would sell – by volume, price, and mix?
- Are we executing the marketing and selling tactics, activities, and tasks as we said we would do?
- Are any changes to marketing, sales, or channel plans required?
- Is there any reason to revisit strategy?

The answers to the above questions, and the outcome of the review of the external environment, provide a more complete understanding of the demand side of the business. With this well-rounded understanding, the demand plan actions, activities, events, assumptions, and numbers should be updated to reflect the current reality. Some companies may call the quantitative demand plan numbers a forecast. Other companies call it a *request for product*. By whatever name, the updated demand plan is communicated to the supply organization and finance group so they can update their plans.

Ross stops talking. He looks around the room to see whether people have questions or whether their expressions show concern. The team members appear quiet and comfortable. Clearly he is "plowing old ground" for those who have implemented S&OP before.

"Let's talk about the Supply Review," Ross says.

He explains that the updated demand plan is used by the supply organization to prepare for the Supply Review. The objective of supply planning is to make every reasonable attempt to support the changes in the demand plan, given the current and anticipated capabilities and resources while optimizing costs and resources. If the volume, timing, quality, and cost targets cannot be achieved in responding to the projected demand, the supply organization develops alternative scenarios. The alternative scenarios typically include requests for changing resources, which may require approval of the leadership team in the Management Business Review.

The Supply Review also serves as the operational performance review for the full supply organization. As part of the operational performance review, the following questions should be asked and answered:

- Are we doing what we said we were going to do?
- Are we on target with our strategic initiatives?
- Is there any reason for us to change our supply strategy?

Ross stops again and surveys the room. The team does not appear to have any questions, which does not surprise him. The team members are experienced with Sales and Operations Planning. Ross expects that they know the fundamentals and concepts of the process, even though there may be some flaws in executing the process in each division.

"Now, let's take a look at the Financial Appraisal. After the Product Management Review, Demand Review, and Supply Review, the finance group consolidates the financial projections and reviews the financial performance to date. The finance group also evaluates the projections to *make sure the numbers are real and the projections are realistic*, as one client CFO states it.

The finance group also compares the changes to the financial plan with the business goals and objectives. It is not unusual for someone from the finance group to sit in on the Product Management Review, Demand Review, and Supply Review. This provides a context for their analysis and evaluation.

The output of the financial appraisal is an input into the next step of the Sales and Operations Planning process, which is Integrated Reconciliation.

"Let's shift our attention to Integrated Reconciliation," Ross says, waving the red light from the pointer across the visual.

He explains that issues will surface from the other elements of the Sales and Operations Planning process that require cross-functional collaboration to resolve. That is one of the primary purposes of Integrated Reconciliation.

It is worrisome when no issues surface. It may mean that only a cursory look is being given to the latest projections and updates. When issues are not being raised, it usually means that questions, which should be asked and answered in each step of the process, are being ignored.

Ross emphasizes that every business is dynamic. Market conditions change. Customer needs and expectations change. Internal and external capabilities change. When cross-functional plans cannot be realigned as change occurs, those issues should be addressed through Integrated Reconciliation. Integrated Reconciliation occurs continuously throughout the month. In large complex organizations, companies are beginning to establish a full-time function in support of Integrated Reconciliation.

The participants in the Integrated Reconciliation process should attempt to resolve the issues without elevating them to the Management Business Review. This principle is frequently defined as resolving issues at the lowest practical level.

Bailey raises her hand. "Ross, it sounds like the Integrated Reconciliation activity is both ongoing throughout the monthly cycle, but also has a scheduled review meeting. Is that correct?" she asks.

Ross responds by explaining that Integrated Reconciliation is a critical element of Integrated Business Planning, especially in larger company implementations. Integrated Reconciliation helps to ensure that issues are resolved at the appropriate level in the business.

Not all issues need to be brought before the leadership team. When issues can be resolved through cross-functional collaboration without executive management intervention, frequently, better solutions are determined and teamwork improves. The participants in Integrated Reconciliation teach each other about their individual aspects of operating the business.

The Integrated Reconciliation process is also used to address nearer-term issues that emerge during the monthly process. It is also used to ensure that each step of the review process has addressed congruency to strategy.

Ross meets Bailey's eyes. "That's the long way of saying that you are correct, Bailey. "Integrated Reconciliation can occur at any point in the monthly S&OP process and culminates in a formal meeting in which options for addressing unresolved issues or gaps are discussed. In this meeting, the team reaches consensus on issues and recommendations that need to be elevated to the Management Business Review. The team also reaches consensus on the proposed agenda for the Management Business Review."

Janis thrusts her hand in the air. "Integrated Reconciliation is a major part of our Sales and Operations Planning process. It has enabled us to move into Stage 4, Strategic Management. And you're right, Ross. The communications involved in problem solving and preventing problems has helped strengthen the management team at the level immediately below the executive leadership team."

Ross starts to speak, but Janis is not finished. She becomes introspective. "We implemented all of the elements of Sales and Operations Planning, but we haven't been as disciplined in asking and answering questions about strategy that you pointed out. This is something we need to improve," she says.

"I'm glad that you can see what is being done well and what may need to be improved," Ross replies. "Let's move to the Management Business Review, then talk some more about applying the basic fundamentals of Sales and Operations Planning at Global Products and Services."

Ross describes the typical situation going into the monthly Management Business Review. Some issues have been discovered and resolved. Other issues have been identified, but require leadership guidance, direction, or decisions. These issues are addressed in the Management Business Review. During the Management Business Review, the updated state of the business is shared among the leadership team.

The leadership team's approach to the Management Business Review should be to strive to find and address issues early. Addressing issues earlier, rather than later, prevents the issues from becoming more complicated. There is time to think the options through and find an optimal solution. There are also, usually, multiple options or alternatives available to address the issue.

In contrast, when issues are addressed later, the advantage of time is taken away and is replaced by urgency. The need for last-minute decisions usually means that fewer options are available, and the options are more difficult and costly to execute.

Mark decides to chime in. "This, of course, requires the leadership team to focus its attention beyond this quarter or this year. It needs to learn to think over the full planning horizon. The leadership wants visibility of gaps to goals and objectives early so that they can be identified and acted upon.

Ross advances the PowerPoint slide. He stares at the screen for a moment, which shows a picture of the actor, Al Pacino. (See Figure 19.)

I want you
to bring me
the answers
before
I ask the
questions.

Al Pacino
as Willy Bank in Ocean's Thirteen

Figure 19 The Essence of Integrated Business Planning From a Leader's Perspective
(Copyright Oliver Wight International. Reproduced with permission.)

Ross turns back to the group and asks. "Has anyone watched the movie, *Ocean's Thirteen?*" Bailey and Janis nod their heads "Yes."

"Remember the character, Willie Bank, the Las Vegas casino operator? He was played by Al Pacino. Bailey and Janis, do you remember Willie Bank saying, "I want you to bring me the answers before I ask the questions?"

Both Bailey and Janis smile their acknowledgement.

Janis laughs, and says, "I know where you're going with this example, Ross. You're saying that's what the leadership team should expect in our Management Business Review."

Ross smiles in return and quickly appraises Janis. She always was smart and quick; still is.

"Ah, Janis. You're so very right," Ross says.

He takes the opportunity to explain that key issues must be made visible to the leadership team. A curtain or veil should not be used to cover up issues that are significant to the business.

The Management Business Review is not the forum for discovering key issues. The discovery process is through each element of the S&OP/IBP process, leading up to the Management Business Review. The focus of the Management Business Review should be decision making and direction setting. Information that sheds light on the current situation, the options, and recommendations should be prepared in advance and discussed in the Management Business Review.

"Just like Willie Bank said, the answers to the executives' questions should be brought to the Management Business Review," Ross says.

Bailey squirms in her seat. She is impatient to address connecting the Sales and Operations Planning process to execution. "I think we all have a pretty good picture of the fundamental process. But how does this help us connect to execution?" she asks.

Mark holds up a hand to Ross, signaling that he would like to respond to Bailey's question. "It is good that we have had a refresher on the basic process because I want us to reach consensus that we will continue to support the fundamental process going forward," Mark says. "Does everyone concur with the basic process that Ross just presented?"

Ross quickly adds, "Please remember that what I just presented took the management and leadership team two days to work through during the original implementation. You've just received a very high-level synopsis to make sure we are all on the same page."

Taylor scoots his seat back to stretch. He says, "I agree with what Janis said. I don't recall the focus on strategy in our education sessions eight years ago. This must be a new emphasis, Ross. But it makes sense to include a strategic element in each step of the process every month. I am not sure we do that now, or if we do, it is more by happenstance than a conscious part of each review."

Taylor scans his teammates. They are nodding their agreement. "I agree with the fundamental process that Ross described, Mark. I just wanted to point out that we have work to do to incorporate strategy into each step of the process."

"Does anyone else have observations to make?" Mark asks. "Any disagreements with the basic process steps?"

The group is silent. "I am about to declare consensus on the fundamental process," Mark says. "Going … going … done!"

Chapter 7

Connection to Execution

THE TEAM TOOK A WELL-NEEDED break, many going outside to get some fresh air before returning to the meeting room. Ross stayed behind to review the remaining material and to ponder the best way to lead the discussion about connecting Integrated Business Planning to execution.

People were quiet as they took their seats, seeing that Ross was in a contemplative mood. Ross looked up to find everyone looking at him expectantly.

"We want to discuss connection to execution now," Ross says to the group. "Then we will explore another model for integrated planning and discuss implementation."

He picks up the remote control and advances to the next slide. "Look at this model," he says. He steps to the screen and points at the slide. (See Figure 20.)

"We showed this model earlier today," he says. "But I've added some explanation to it. The model clearly depicts that there are a whole lot of things going on inside the company at a more detailed level below the S&OP process."

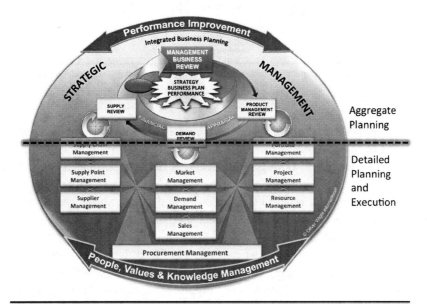

Figure 20 Integrated Business Model (Copyright Oliver Wight International. Reproduced with permission.)

Ross advances the PowerPoint presentation. "Now look at this model. It should be familiar to most of you, as we discussed it during the original S&OP implementation eight years ago."

Ross explains that the model was affectionately called the "plumbing chart" as it depicts information flowing through all the arrows. (See Figure 21.)

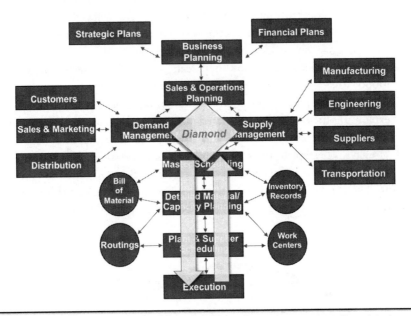

Figure 21 Enterprise Integration Model (Copyright Oliver Wight International. Reproduced with permission.)

Ross notes that the plumbing chart model is less appropriate in illustrating Integrated Business Planning since it is primarily oriented around the supply chain. The model reviewed earlier (Figure 20) includes the same management and communication processes, but is more complete from a <u>business enterprise</u> point of view.

"Let's explore the plumbing chart in some detail. It shows the connectivity from Sales and Operations Planning to detailed planning and execution in the supply chain," Ross says.

He asks the group to note where Sales and Operations Planning connects to Demand Management, Supply Management, and Master Supply Planning (Figure 21). Both Demand Management and Supply Management have aggregate and detailed components to them. Sales and Operations Planning integrates the information at the aggregate level. Master Supply Scheduling, which is sometimes referred to as Master Production Scheduling, or simply Master Scheduling, integrates the aggregate information at the detailed level. This part of the plumbing chart model has sometimes been referred to as the "Diamond."

Nolan raises his hand. "Ross, why is Master Production Scheduling now referred to as Master Supply Scheduling? What has changed?" he asks.

"Business models have changed," Ross replies.

He explains that, today, it is unusual _not_ to outsource the manufacture of products, yet companies still need to plan for the supply of those products. Also, the integrated planning model is increasingly being deployed by service industries. This makes the term Master Planning more relevant to more companies.

Ross goes on to explain that John Proud, the author of the widely respected book, *Master Scheduling*, still prefers the acronym, MPS. But he has changed the description to Master Planning and Scheduling.

"I particularly like Master Supply Planning and Scheduling," Ross comments. "It applies whether companies are making or buying a product or delivering a service."

Ross shows another slide. (See Figure 22.) "Even as the S&OP process has evolved, so has the detailed planning and scheduling processes. Take a look at this Integrated Planning and Control model," he says. "It adds some additional perspective to the work ahead of Bailey and her team. We simply do not have time to discuss this model in more detail during this session. That will have to be part of Bailey's work.

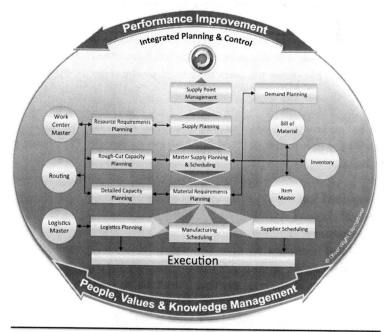

Figure 22 Integrated Planning and Control Model
(Copyright Oliver Wight International. Reproduced with permission.)

Bailey raises her hand and says, "Whatever you call it and whatever model you use to show it, this level of supply planning is supported by aggregate information from the S&OP or IBP process. It is also supported with detailed information from both Demand and Supply Planning. Is that right?"

"You are correct," Ross replies. "So which should you do; top-down aggregate planning or bottom-up detailed planning?"

The room is quiet for a moment. Janis, always quick thinking, smiles and responds; "Why, both, of course. We learned that in the previous implementation. We use detailed information in the near term and aggregate it up. We use aggregate information in the outer time periods. In the Management Business Review, we look primarily at the aggregate information. But in the other steps of the process, we will likely need to look at more detailed information in the near term and aggregate information further out in the planning horizon."

Nolan thinks about the software tool implications of doing both detailed and aggregate planning. "If that's the case, then we need a database and software tools to enable people to aggregate and disaggregate the data," he says. "I now understand why the S&OP database draws from our Enterprise Resource Planning systems in the near term and often uses aggregate planning from another source when the detailed data is not available for aggregation in the ERP system, particularly in the outer planning horizon."

"That's a good observation, Nolan," Ross responds. He explains that, ideally, the detailed data needs to extend across the planning horizon long enough to encompass key decision points or lead times, such as cumulative lead times. Detailed information is not usually necessary over the entire S&OP/IBP planning horizon.

Ross turns toward the computer and clicks the remote control to advance the slide presentation. He allows the team time to study the chart on the slide. (See Figure 23.)

"Let me explain what this chart depicts," Ross says.

He tells the group that detailed information to support the master plan and schedule includes:

- Item-level forecast
- Actual demand
- The master schedule or supply plan
- On-hand inventory
- Calculations for projected available inventory balance
- Calculations of the quantity that is available to promise

"Most ERP software supports this information, but many companies don't have the disciplined processes to keep the information accurate and current," Ross says.

Period = Weeks	1	2	3	4	5	6	7	8
Forecast	20	20	20	20	20	20	20	20
Actual Demand								
Projected Available Balance	20	0	40	80	60	40	20	0
Available to Promise								
Supply Planning			60	60				

On Hand: 40

Order Qty: 60

Valid Promising = Available to Promise and Abnormal Demand Management
Stability = Forecast Consumption and Firm Planned Orders
Managing Change = Action Messages and Communication

Figure 23 Detailed Demand/Supply/Inventory Review (Master Plan and Schedule)
(Copyright Oliver Wight International. Reproduced with permission.)

He cites on-hand inventory balances, due dates, and customer orders as data that are frequently not kept accurate by many companies. Without the discipline to keep data accurate and current, the detailed plans become unsynchronized and untrustworthy. Incorrect data impact the integrity and credibility of the master schedule, supplier schedules, and production schedules. When data is not accurate or out of date, people don't trust the plan, and additional work is created to validate the data in the system. At worst, planners stop using the ERP system and begin planning the business outside the system.

Nolan raises his hand. "There's another issue, Ross," he says. "Some ERP software has the data you have shown, but it isn't in the form of the combined, integrated chart we see in your slide. The data exists on separate screens, which makes it difficult to mentally put all the information together."

Nolan's comment stirs Mark's memory of the initial implementation at the Universal Products division. He tells the group that until they established the discipline to keep data accurate, the division did not achieve the full benefits of implementing the S&OP process. "It was frustrating," Mark says. "We had approved, aligned plans through the S&OP process, but we struggled to plan and execute at the detailed level because the data in the system was wrong. And, Nolan, you're right about the problem of the data in the chart not being available in one screen at the item level. We had to change the report structure to remedy that problem. It wasn't a major task, but it needed to be done."

"Mark's observations are correct about the frustration when plans align at the aggregate level, but there is difficulty in planning and executing at the detailed level," Ross says, advancing the presentation to the next slide.

Ross explains that it is all too common to have a well-operating Sales and Operations Planning or Integrated Business Planning process that is not supported by equally effective supporting processes. When this situation exists, companies continue to struggle to improve their operational and financial performance.

"That is why we are pushing hard today to get companies to include the *connection* to the next level of detail in their Integrated Business Planning implementations," Ross says.

Mark looks around the table and sees heads nodding in recognition of the point Ross has made.

"Okay, team," he says. "I think this calls for a consensus. I suggest that we have a consensus that this IBP project includes connecting the output of S&OP to the next level of detail required to drive execution. Any comments?"

"Just one," Bailey says. "The next level of detail that we have today may not provide the amount of detail required for execution. Greater levels of detail will be required. And those levels of detail will be included in the detailed planning and control and supply chain project work. Agreed?"

The group is quiet, thinking about Bailey's statement.

Ross advances the presentation, searching for a slide.

"This slide may help," he says. "This is a simplified look at the multiple levels of planning information."

He points out the aggregate level of information for Sales and Operations Planning or Integrated Business Planning and the first level of detailed demand, supply, and product information to support Master Supply Planning and Scheduling. (See Figure 24.) He uses the laser pointer to highlight the third level of detail.

"There's another level of detail that may be needed to support scheduling for the supply planning side of the business," Ross comments.

Mark scans the room. People appear to be comfortable. "Bailey's statement is correct about needing another level of detail for execution, and those detailed processes will be addressed in the supply chain project. With this recognition, do we have consensus to include the next level of demand and supply detail planning in the IBP project?"

As one, the group responds with, "Yes!"

Mark nods in satisfaction. "Good. Let's move on," he says.

"Let me have the floor for a minute before we go on, please," Taylor says. "I want to make sure we don't miss a key point." Taylor points out that Strategic Planning is an aggregate planning process, and the next level of detail is the aggregate

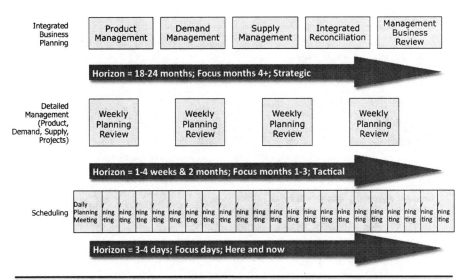

Figure 24 Planning and Scheduling Processes (Copyright Oliver Wight International. Reproduced with permission.)

level of information that supports the S&OP/IBP process. It is important to remember that there are different levels of aggregation depending upon the management process involved. The last visual Ross showed is aimed at the supply chain. Much, if not most, of strategy is not really about supply chain. It is about markets and customers, product, or the development of value propositions. It is about product portfolio management.

"The information addressed in the Management Business Review needs to be at a level that helps ensure we are executing the strategy. Isn't that right?" Taylor asks.

"Once again, Taylor, you make a good point that needs to be well understood. Take a look at this visual," Ross says.

He advances to the next slide (Figure 25).

"Does this help?" Ross asks, allowing the team to study the chart. "You might use a logic statement and say that the S&OP/IBP process is to Strategy as Master Planning is to S&OP/IBP. Make sense?"

"I am definitely okay as long as everyone else agrees with that principle," Taylor says.

"It makes sense to me," Mark says, turning to the group. "Do we all agree?"

Heads nod, as one, in agreement.

Ross looks at the time on his cell phone and glances to the back of the room where the snacks and drinks have been refreshed.

"I think we should take a break," he says. "Let's all return in 15 minutes, please."

Ross notices a message on his cell phone. He recognizes the phone number and decides to step out of the room to return the call.

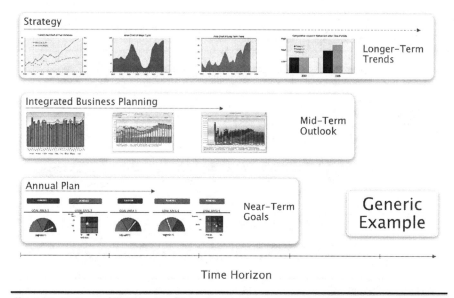

Figure 25 Strategy and S&OP Become "Naturally Linked" Via Integrated and Aligned Measurement
(Copyright Oliver Wight International. Reproduced with permission.)

Listening to the message, Ross is happy to hear from the new president of a services company. He had wondered when John might call.

John's message is right to the point. His services company needs to implement Integrated Business Planning immediately. Business is rapidly growing, and the company is struggling to economically ramp up to support the growth.

Ross recalls helping John implement Integrated Business Planning at a manufacturing company several years ago. John's management team moved the process through all four stages of implementation and truly had an Integrated Business Planning process linked to Strategic Management.

"I needed a new challenge, as you know, Ross, which is why I moved to lead a services business. What I am seeing here is that all of the principles of Integrated Business Planning will apply to a services business, just like it did with a manufacturing business. I'd appreciate your calling me back to discuss how we might get started with an implementation."

Ross jots a note to himself to call John this evening and walks to the back of the room to get a bottle of water before returning to the session.

Chapter 8

Integrated Business Planning As the Primary Way to Manage the Business

THE TEAM MEMBERS ARE IN their seats and looking eager to move forward.

Without preamble, Ross advances to the next slide (Figure 26), the fundamental, monthly IBP cycle. He asks the group to take a moment to review the slide, which is now becoming more familiar. (See Figure 26.)

Figure 26 Fundamental Integrated Business Planning Monthly Cycle
(Copyright Oliver Wight International. Reproduced with permission.)

"It looks much like the S&OP model we used eight years ago; but, after our conversation today, seems somewhat different to me," Janis comments.

"That's good, Janis," Ross replies. "You know one of my favorite quotes attributed to George Box, the mathematician, and to Albert Einstein is: 'All models are wrong; some are useful.' It's a model that we at Effective Management Inc. use to stimulate discussion and specific process design for individual companies."

Ross advances to the next slide. He explains that the model shown on the slide (Figure 27) has helped to better illustrate the integration of business processes when IBP is used to truly manage the business.

"As we have discussed multiple times today, this leadership process integrates horizontally across the functions and vertically between leadership and management," Ross says.

Figure 27 Integration of Business Processes When Integrated Business Planning Is Used to Truly Manage the Business (Copyright Oliver Wight International. Reproduced with permission.)

"So I have a question for you, Ross, and you, Mark," Janis says. "If this is a process to manage the entire business, where are the functions of strategic assessment and development, information technology, human resources, risk management, legal, public relations, facilities, and other processes within the company? We found, at Universal Products, that we needed to include those functions in our S&OP process, or we would find surprises and constraints to our performance. Where are they in your model?"

Mark responds. "Without a monthly cadence that includes these elements, the executive team does not have a full view of the condition and needs of the business," he says. "Review of these functions or activities is needed to have the full picture of the business."

"You said earlier today that IBP was not vastly different from Sales and Operations Planning; but if these elements are included or implied in this model, it is more comprehensive than traditional S&OP," Janis observes.

Ross points in succession to the Product Management Review, Demand Review, Supply Review, Financial Appraisal, and Management Business Review. "They're still in the Integrated Business Planning model," he says. "The other elements are also processes in any business. During implementation, specifically in the design sessions, our clients strive to ensure that these other elements of business management are connected and integrated. In most companies, these elements are managed in different, often non-integrated, meetings. Sometimes they are part of the leadership team's monthly "staff" meeting. Sometimes they are part of a functional review. The key is that they get viewed and reviewed in an integrated manner. That way, cause and effect can be understood in decision making, especially when making decisions on resources and priorities."

Ross glances around the room. The team members continue to study the Integrated Business Planning model.

Taylor asks, "So where are they on the model?"

"Before I answer your question directly, Taylor, let me share with you how companies are transitioning to Integrated Business Planning. It will help you to understand the inclusion of the other elements into IBP," Ross says.

Ross explained that first, and foremost, companies must get their basic processes in order. He reminds the group of the Integrated Business Planning maturity chart that was shown earlier. It is imperative that demand, supply, and inventory are regularly and routinely balanced in an enterprise. Without this alignment, the leadership team's time is spent dealing with chaos and problems, rather than the opportunities for the business.

As a company progresses through the maturity stages, the chaos recedes, and the business is more completely under control. When this point in maturity is reached, the leadership team is able to work more on opportunities and risk mitigation, simply because they have more time to do so.

"We have clearly seen that at Universal Products," Mark says. "One of the biggest benefits from a personal perspective was the freeing up of time to do positive, interesting, and fun activities."

Janis laughs, "Fun?"

Ross continues his explanation. He tells the group that, to the extent possible, companies should keep the IBP model as simple as practical, which is not always possible in a large, highly complex business. To the extent that the other elements Janis mentioned can be included in each step of the process, this should be done.

"A simple example is strategy," Ross says. "As we have previously discussed, each step should have an agenda item specifically related to execution of strategy for that function. The Integrated Reconciliation process and Integrated Reconciliation Review are also places where strategic issues or topics should be surfaced."

"Another example is Human Resources," Ross continues.

He explains that since the human resource function is a service to the other company functions, it should be connected to each step of the process. If there are issues that can't be resolved during the individual process steps, then there is an avenue through the Integrated Reconciliation process to work towards resolution quickly. If resolution cannot be reached, then the issue should be addressed in the Integrated Reconciliation Review or the Management Business Review.

"Some companies may modify the model to more closely match their organization and accountability structure," Ross says. "I'll remind you that we recommend to always keep the model as simple as practical, but adding other functional steps to the model sometimes adds clarity."

Ross explains that the model shows financial analysis and implies a work step where the financial information is consolidated and analyzed in preparation for Integrated Reconciliation. Some companies wish to show this as a separate step to ensure clarity of accountability for the financial analysis and review. Often the executive accountable for Integrated Reconciliation is someone other than the CFO, and this model is intended to clearly show that the CFO is actively involved in the process.

Janis, thinking about the financial role, speaks up. "But your model calls it Integrated Reconciliation. The word "reconciliation" has a financial connotation to it," she observes.

"Here's something to consider, Janis," Ross says, smiling at her. "This is a complete business reconciliation, not just a financial reconciliation. The finance function clearly plays an important role, but is not the sole participant. Nor is this review just about financial performance. It is about total business performance, operationally and financially."

Nolan, who has been quiet during most of the conversation, speaks up. "I have heard of this referred to as a multiple review process," he comments. "What you are saying is that, in some instances, IBP processes might have different numbers of reviews?"

"That's right," Ross acknowledges. "It is really a multi-review process. Remember, all models are wrong; some are useful. The work gets done either way. One implementation issue is how a company chooses to address the Financial Appraisal and Review in the individual process design."

Ross goes on to explain that when companies have incorporated a Financial Review into their Integrated Business Planning processes, it does not mean this is a large meeting. The Financial Review is a culmination of all of the financial appraisal activities that occur within each individual review as part of the Integrated Business Planning process. It may be attended by as few as two people, the chief financial officer and the Financial Review lead (who is often a controller). Depending on the size and organizational structure of a company, the Financial Review could also include cross-functional representatives.

Ross encourages clients to have a small team of a few players in the Financial Review, rather than a larger group of participants from various company functions. The Integrated Reconciliation Review is designed to deal with the business issues that surface from all the reviews, including the Financial Appraisal and Review.

"So what happens in the Financial Appraisal and Review?" Janis asks.

Ross replies that the purpose of the Financial Appraisal and Review is to determine what the latest consolidated projections mean financially to the company. The changes to the latest projections should be analyzed. The latest projections represent truth, as it is known today.

This truth should be compared to the quarterly and annual financial commitments that the company has made to the board of directors and/or Wall Street. If there are gaps between the latest projections and the quarterly and annual financial commitments, these gaps should be identified. The impact of the gaps to the business should be made visible to the leadership team through the Integrated Reconciliation Review and Management Business Review. The Financial Appraisal and Review could be looked at as a preparatory step for the Integrated Reconciliation Review and the Management Business Review.

Ross pauses and scans the team members. Most are nodding their heads to indicate they understand.

"Let's talk about some of the other areas, sometimes referred to as support functions, sometimes as infrastructure and administration." Ross says.

Bailey comments, half in jest, "Almost always referred to as G&A, or general and administrative; overhead at budget time."

Ross advances to the next slide. The slide depicts an organization chart with the support functions that are often considered Business Administration highlighted. (See Figure 28.)

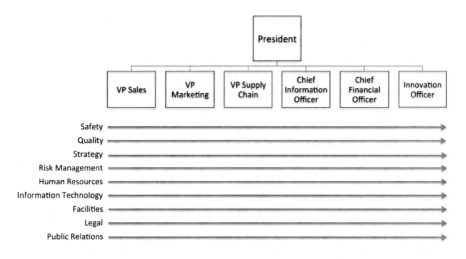

Figure 28 Support Functions That <u>May</u> Be Included in the Integrated Business Planning Process
(Copyright Oliver Wight International. Reproduced with permission.)

Ross explains that the support or infrastructure-administration input certainly should be reviewed in each process review for that function. But in more mature processes, there is a regular review of the functions required to support the effective performance of the *entire* business entity.

These functions include, as a minimum, information technology, human resources, facilities, security, legal, and public relations. It could include risk management if it is a separate function. It could include quality and regulatory affairs. It should include other key functions that are deemed of key importance by the leadership team. The purpose of this support or Infrastructure-Administration Review is to ensure that all the support functions surface issues and opportunities that need to be addressed to ensure the company achieves its strategic and business objectives.

Janis struggles to understand the Infrastructure-Administration Review and how it would work at Global Products and Services, Inc. She seems to speak for the group when she asks, "Many of those infrastructure and administration functions often report to or through the CFO. Are you suggesting a new reporting structure?"

"Not necessarily," Ross replies.

He points out that the Integrated Business Planning chart is a process model, not an organization chart. It is meant to recognize that the business administration functions or activities are often neglected in reviewing the state of the business. They typically are not included as part of a company's traditional Financial Appraisal and Review. Rather than being viewed as key assets necessary to manage the business, they are often viewed simply as overhead, failing to really understand their significance and importance to the other functions. Yet, these functions and activities need a forum for addressing issues and opportunities – because these functions impact the performance and health of a business.

Looking towards Janis, Ross acknowledges her concern. "In some companies, these functions do not report to the finance organization, but that depends upon the size and complexity of the business."

Nolan has been thinking about how a Support/Infrastructure-Administration Review could impact his Information Technology organization and his responsibilities. He senses opportunity for his organization with the addition of the Infrastructure-Administration monthly review and wants Ross to confirm whether his thinking is correct.

"You all know that the Information Technology group is perpetually criticized for being non-responsive and too expensive. Yet when we develop the budgets every year, the leadership team seems to always view the IT group as the first place to cut expenses and reduce overhead."

Nolan scans the team members. No one argues with his statement, and a few have sheepish expressions on their faces.

He continues by asking, "Ross, are you saying that a disciplined monthly review will provide a regular and routine forum to address resource and investment issues and priorities?"

"Absolutely," Ross responds. "That is exactly what I am saying."

Nolan leans back in his chair and pumps his fist in the air. "That's great; excellent in fact! This forum has been needed for a long time."

"Please note that I have not said how to connect this review to the integrated process. The simplest approach would be to bring issues to the IR by exception, and that could surely work for many companies. Others might wish to have additional reviews in the monthly process, depending upon the degree of strategic importance to the enterprise and how the enterprise has chosen to organize."

Ross wants to direct the group's attention back to Janis's question on organizational structure. He wants them to think in terms of how the Integrated Business Planning process could be structured at Global Products and Services, Inc.

"I want to give you something to think about with regard to organizational structure and the operation of Integrated Business Planning," he says.

He asks the group to think about the person in charge of the business, such as the chief executive officer, president, chief operating officer, or general manager. They might desire to have one person responsible for each of the respective reviews in the Integrated Business Planning process depicted in the model from his or her perspective. If this should occur, the process reviews would mirror organizational responsibility.

"This approach has some advantages." Ross states. "It provides clarity of accountability from a top-down perspective. But in reality, how the accountabilities for Integrated Business Planning are structured is highly dependent upon the size and complexity of the business. In smaller companies, individuals most often have multiple accountabilities in this IBP model."

Bailey works through her mind how flexible or fixed the design of the Integrated Business Planning process needs to be at Global Products and Services, Inc. She wonders what Ross might recommend.

"Are you recommending a fixed IBP model, Ross, or could it have more or fewer reviews, depending upon the organization?"

Bailey holds up her hand to stop Ross from replying. "Before you answer, let me explain why I asked the question," she says.

She turns to her team members and points out that the Sales and Operations Planning process that has been deployed helped Global Products clarify roles, responsibilities, and accountabilities. The deployment of Sales and Operations Planning compelled the divisions to address the lack of clarity of roles, responsibilities, and accountabilities in several functional areas of the business. From the general manager's perspective, or Person In Charge (PIC), as Ross would say, Sales and Operations Planning made it easy to assign accountability because one person was made accountable for each review, and this accountability matched the structure of the organization.

"As you know, we even created titles of Vice President of Demand and Vice President of Supply in Universal Products," Bailey says.

The team members look on with interest, and Bailey continues, " If there is some flexibility in the number of reviews, then the Integrated Business Planning process structure could be made to match the accountabilities and the organization. What are your thoughts on this idea, Ross?"

Ross smiles his appreciation at Bailey's perceptiveness.

"Bailey, you are absolutely correct. Inside Effective Management, Inc., my colleagues and I have wrestled with that very issue in discussing the practical application of the IBP model."

Ross shares some of Effective Management, Inc.'s conclusions from those discussions. The reviews need to happen for effective and efficient management. How the reviews are depicted in the graphical Integrated Business Planning model is probably less important than the fact that all the reviews are conducted each month and that accountability is clear.

He gives an example of how one client structured its Integrated Business Planning process. Effective risk management was critical for this client. The person heading up the risk management function reported directly to the president. The client included Risk Management in each process review and also conducted a separate review that consolidated all the key risks from an overall perspective in their Integrated Business Planning process.

For another client, most of its manufacturing is outsourced to companies in Asia and China. The timing of deliveries and the cost of transportation are critical for customer service and achieving gross margin objectives. This client wanted improved integration to reduce the hundreds of thousands of dollars they spent each month on express freight costs. The client included a separate Logistics Review in its Integrated Business Planning process. The Logistics Review followed and was closely tied to the Supply Review.

Another client in the high-tech industry added a high-level Market Review prior to the Demand Review. The accelerated pace of change in the high-tech industry is opening new markets for this client. The company's leadership wanted to be ahead of, or at least in sync with, the innovation curve, not lag it. So the client added a Market Review to their structure of the Integrated Business Planning process. This is normally done as part of the Demand Review in most companies and as an input to the PMR; but strategically, the Market Review was viewed as being so important to the entire business, they wanted accountability and visibility directly to the Leadership Team and the Person In Charge.

"In my view, it is absolutely okay to structure IBP to match how the leadership team desires to manage and structure the business," Ross says.

Ross walks to the screen and points at the standard Integrated Business Planning model (Figure 26). "This model is designed to help people clarify and understand the Integrated Business Planning process. It is not the ultimate process structure for all companies in all situations," he says.

The group is quiet. Ross wonders if they understand or need further clarification. Before he can ask the group, Janis speaks up.

"Ross, let me explain what I think I heard," she says. "The standard reviews for Integrated Business Planning are Product and Portfolio, Demand, Supply, and Financial Appraisal as a precursor to Integrated Reconciliation."

Janis explains that Integrated Reconciliation has grown in significance as the S&OP process has evolved into IBP. The IBP process culminates in the Management Business Review, or MBR. Some companies, depending upon their size, complexity, and organization, may wish to add reviews to the process structure. This does not negate the need for, or the sequence of, the five fundamental reviews.

Janis pauses to take a breath of air.

"When we went through our original education for Sales and Operations Planning," she continues, "you emphasized how much time should be required by the business leader, the Person In Charge, when the process is working well. If I can quote you, you said that the Person In Charge should expect to be in full control of the business within four hours or less each month. Right?"

Before Ross can respond, Mark adds, "That's what Ross told us; and, in the Universal Product division, it evolved to where the Management Business Review took two hours to conduct each month."

Janis turns to look at Mark.

"I'm not challenging the original statement, but I do have a question about added reviews, if they are deemed to be necessary," she says. "Should the expectation be that the MBR is still four hours or less? Or will it take longer with the addition of output from additional reviews?"

Ross has made the bold claim that company leaders can be in full control of the business with an investment of four hours of time each month. In the last few years, he has softened his position, however. He is going to need to explain why he has altered his position on this subject.

He looks first at Janis and then Mark before saying, "I have had a few clients over the past few years that have fully embraced the principle of using the IBP process as *the primary process of running the business*. All, or virtually all, the management meetings previously held separately were incorporated into the IBP process and, more specifically, fed into the Integrated Reconciliation Review and Management Business Review."

Ross explains that issues are surfaced and addressed in the appropriate functional reviews each month. Issues requiring cross-functional discussions, leadership guidance, or leadership decisions are addressed in the Integrated Reconciliation Review and, in some cases as necessary, they are elevated to the Management Business Review. As a result, the agenda for the Management Business Review is more extensive than when the process has only demand and supply chain focus. That means the MBR may take longer, at times, than four hours. The additional time is more than offset through elimination of other meetings that are redundant, frequently lack integration, and are no longer necessary.

Ross points out to the group another factor that extends the time needed to conduct the Management Business Review. With the volatility and uncertainty of the recent economic times, many leadership teams are reviewing more scenarios and contingency plans. Reviews of scenarios are essential to effectively managing the business, making the right decisions, and being prepared when business conditions change.

While the review of scenarios and contingency plans takes more time in the Management Business Review, the leadership and management teams are better prepared to pull the trigger on changes needed to respond to different business conditions. The investment in additional time up front reduces chaos and the unproductive time spent responding and reacting to surprises.

Ross looks at Janis. "My explanation is the long way to respond to your question," he says. "The short answer is that I expect the Management Business Review will use up all four hours if there is more content added from other regular and routine reviews. In some cases, it could take longer. I've seen some clients take a full day, or two half days, depending upon the meeting styles and culture of the company."

Ross tells the group about a client with revenue of $8 billion that was deploying a massive change of strategy. This change of strategy involved a new primary value proposition, a change in technology, a restructure of the organization and compensation programs, and even the change of the company's name and brand. The timetable for this extensive change was less than a year.

The company used the Integrated Business Planning process as a strategic management process. The Management Business Review took two full days each month.

"So, I think the answer is that it takes whatever time it takes," Ross says. "The client example I just shared is an extremely unusual case. In general, I still expect that most Management Business Reviews will take six hours or less."

Mark understands the point that the Management Business Review should take whatever time it takes to address the issues, provide guidance, and make decisions. He is confused about when to potentially add reviews and does not want Ross to move on to other topics before helping him better understand specifically when there might be a separate Strategy Review.

"Ross, I know we probably need to move on in the interest of time, but I don't understand why there might be a separate Strategy Review," Marks says. "Here's what confuses me. You have already said that strategy is reviewed in each step of the process. You have also said that IBP is a strategic management process. And now you are saying we could need a monthly Strategy Review prior to, and in preparation for, the MBR."

Ross is quick to respond. "Let me explain the rationale."

He tells the group that, in practice, most mature Sales and Operations Planning processes incorporate strategy in each of the reviews. Strategy is an agenda item in each review as appropriate.

The purpose of the Strategy Review is to validate that each of the functions is operating within the agreed-upon strategy and to identify whether there are reasons to recommend a change to that strategy. It is also to identify gaps to strategic goals and actions to close the gaps. Further, the purpose is to make sure that strategic initiatives are progressing on scope, on time, and on budget. The review of strategy in each review, by its nature, has a functional view.

There is also a need to review strategy from a corporate perspective, above the division or business unit level. Like the client example, there may be significant strategic changes that encompass the entire company. These changes are beyond what would be reviewed in the individual process reviews in individual business units or individual functions when looking from a higher-level perspective.

Another example of the need for a strategy review, from the corporate perspective, is a strategy of growing sales revenue through mergers and acquisitions. The execution of this strategy would be an item of discussion in a separate Strategy Review.

The corporate review of strategy should not be confused with the strategies that must be reviewed in each functional review. For example, innovation strategy needs to be reviewed in the Product and Portfolio Review. Demand strategies need to be reviewed in the Demand Review. Supply strategies should be reviewed in the Supply Review.

Someone needs to be responsible to make sure all the strategic reviews are completed and that connections between the functions are clearly integrated. This is often accomplished in the Integrated Reconciliation Review. Large companies often have a strategy organization that is accountable for this review. The Strategy Review should occur separately from the Integrated Reconciliation process. Pertinent issues are addressed in the Integrated Reconciliation Review and, ultimately, the Management Business Review, as appropriate.

Taylor, the Vice President of Strategic Planning, has been quiet during the discussion on how strategy is handled in an Integrated Business Planning process. He feels it is time to share his thoughts.

"You may think I have a vested interest in this; and, of course, I do," he says to the group. "I really like the idea of a separate Strategy Review. It further confirms that IBP is a strategic management process, and it will help provide a means to ensure that strategy gets executed."

The group is silent. No one objects to Taylor's statement.

Bailey has a different question. "Can some of the reviews be combined, or do they have to be separate?" she asks.

Ross explains that he does not encourage companies to combine the reviews, especially in an immature process; although he has seen it done. It is important to remember that each functional area is responsible to review and address the plans; the assumptions behind the plans; the assumptions, strategies, tactics, action items, and performance measures in their reviews.

However the company chooses to structure the Integrated Business Planning process, these topics must be fully addressed, and the accountabilities for both developing and executing the plans and addressing the business issues must be well defined.

"For efficiency purposes, I don't have an objection if some of the elements can be combined into one step instead of two steps," Ross says. "But, I must raise a caution. Let's say a change to the plan, tactics, or strategy is agreed upon in one of the functional areas. Understanding the consequences of that change in the next functional area requires preparation time. If two reviews have been combined in one review meeting, you take away that preparation time; and decisions or recommendations are often made without all the facts. If this situation occurs regularly, it indicates that the functional area deserves its own review with time between the reviews to properly prepare."

Ross has been hesitant to discuss higher-level corporate reviews during today's session. His experience has shown that the best functioning Integrated Business Planning processes are based on solid division-level processes. Once the operational and financial information at the division level is credible, then higher-level corporate reviews become more effective and more meaningful. Corporate reviews move beyond just financial reviews and truly provide information to the corporate leadership team for optimizing the entire business, across all the divisions and functions.

Ross plans to revisit this corporate-level discussion in a future session when Jack Baxter, the President, and his management team can be together. There simply is not sufficient time today to properly address this corporate-level IBP process structure with all its nuances and choices.

Given the points raised by Bailey and others today, Ross feels he must at least provide an awareness of a higher-level process framework to the team.

"Team, I feel I must share a few thoughts on IBP from a corporate-level perspective," Ross says.

He explains that today's discussion purposely focused on Integrated Business Planning from a divisional perspective, which is appropriate as the divisions in Global Products are largely independent.

As the company continues to grow, it may find greater potential for integrating opportunities between divisions across the businesses. If and when this situation occurs, higher, corporate-level reviews will be needed as part of the overall IBP process.

Mark and Ross have previously discussed corporate-level reviews during one-on-one conversations. Mark chimes in, "So, if I understand you, Ross, the discussions we have had about the IBP process structure, with the various reviews, have been focused on division-level IBP processes. We may find a time when we want to implement IBP processes from a perspective higher than the divisions. Is that correct?"

"Yes, Mark, you heard right," Ross responds. "But, in order for the higher, corporate-level processes to be more than just financial reviews, there must be solid division-level reviews first. Of course, there will always be some level of corporate financial reviews. The issue is: the better the divisional IBP processes, the more credible the corporate financial reviews will be."

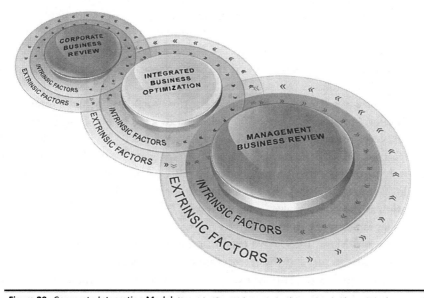

Figure 29 Corporate Integration Model (Copyright Oliver Wight International. Reproduced with permission.)

Ross moves to the computer and brings up a new visual (Figure 29).

"Take a look at this model," Ross says.

Bill jokes, "All models are wrong; some are useful."

Ross smiles. "You are absolutely right, Bill. This is especially true when it comes to a Corporate Integration Model in large, multi-national, multi-divisional, matrix-managed organizations. It is for this reason that we are not going to spend any significant time on this subject today. Jack, Mark, and I have discussed the need for another session similar to this one that focuses specifically on Corporate Integration. However, we agreed to build a stronger set of divisional processes first."

Mark stands. He wants to share a couple of thoughts.

"You will notice the Corporate Integration Model has three elements — Management Business Review, Integrated Business Optimization and, finally, a Corporate Business Review."

He tells the group that he and Jack have discussed the final element of the division IBP processes, the division Management Business Reviews, and provided a logical input to the analytical element of corporate integration, which is integrated business optimization. Integrated business optimization provides a natural feed into the Corporate Business Review.

"From a Global Products process design perspective," Mark says, "we will really need to think through that higher-level corporate process to ensure it provides value-added information and decision making for the enterprise."

Mark's comments trigger a thought from Taylor. "I can see where this really needs to be looked at carefully," Taylor says. "We will need to understand who the key players are, what information is really required at the corporate level, and what decisions will be made at the corporate level rather than the divisional level. It could get quite complex if we are not careful."

Ross decides to bring to an end the conversation about the Corporate Integration Model.

"We have much work to be done at the divisional level before addressing the corporate-level process," he says. "We will need to keep in mind the prospect of a corporate-level process when designing the division-level IBP process. Eventually, the division-level IBP processes will need to integrate with the corporate-level process. In a complex environment, how the processes integrate needs considerable thought. But keep in mind, the corporate-level process will not be successful if the foundation at the division level is not rock solid."

Bailey is not ready to move on yet. She has a question.

"Ross and Mark, I know we need to move on, but I need clarity on another subject. It seems to me that the connection of direction and decisions to the next level of detail, to Master Supply Planning and Scheduling, should not be taken lightly. It is going to require considerable thought and process design work. Am I right? And is this part of Mark's charter?"

Ross looks at Mark and asks, "Do you want to answer Bailey's question?"

"I do," Mark replies. "Bailey, I view the connection to the next level of detail, to Master Supply Planning and Scheduling, a part of the charter for the IBP initiative. I don't view it as my charter or your charter. I see is as *our* charter."

Mark explains that he and Bailey will need to be 100 percent in concert on the process design for connecting Integrated Business Planning to Master Planning and Scheduling. It is part of the charter for the Integrated Business Planning initiative after developing the process design together. Then, the connection can be implemented, in whole or in part, immediately without waiting for improvement in detailed planning software or tools.

"With the Integrated Supply Chain Management initiative, we will probably need some improved software and tools to support some of the detailed planning processes. Tool implementations to support detailed planning and control take much longer to implement than an IBP process. I see the implementation of improved tools for detailed Supply Chain Planning and Control as part of your charter. Do you agree?"

Bailey looks visibly relieved and pleased.

"I agree," she says. "You and I are in sync, Mark."

Ross feels the group has reached a good time for a short break. He also wants to coordinate with Mark the key points to cover before wrapping up the session.

He looks at his watch. "Time for a break. Please be back in ten minutes," he says.

CHAPTER 9

REVISITING CONSENSUS

MARK PULLS ROSS ASIDE AT the break. "What do you think, Ross. Are we on track? Any concerns?" he asks.

Ross doesn't immediately answer. He is taking an inventory, in his mind, about what has been accomplished and what remains to be accomplished.

Finally, he says, "We are on track for the day. I am pleased with how you and Bailey seem to be in alignment about your roles. Taylor has been somewhat quiet this afternoon. He doesn't seem to be resistant, and he is not challenging the principles and concepts that have been discussed. But he wasn't very talkative, either, until just before the break."

"As usual, I think Taylor is a couple of steps ahead of the group," Mark replies. He tells Ross that he talked with Taylor during the last break. Taylor was already thinking about the next steps for developing the process design. He asked Mark his thoughts about the structure of a Strategy Review. He was concerned that some of the individual business units have not assigned a person to be dedicated to developing strategy. That causes him to question how the strategy review process will be built into the monthly process."

He pats Ross on the shoulder. "I've worked with Taylor for years. I guarantee if he was not on board with Integrated Business Planning, he would speak out. He is quiet because he is stewing about how strategy integration should work. I assured Taylor that we won't solve this issue today, but it will be worked out in the workshops that you and your team will facilitate for us."

"I'll make a point of meeting with him the next time I am at headquarters," Ross says. "We can discuss his concerns in detail. I'll reassure him that we will provide coaching support as the project moves forward."

"That's a great idea," Mark replies.

"Do you have any other comments about the day so far?" Ross asks.

"When we were having the last discussion on how the Integrated Business Planning process could be structured, I was wishing I'd had the foresight to bring someone in to be our scribe," Mark says. "Same with documenting the consensus items. I sure hope Bill has kept good notes. We'll have to compare our notes tomorrow while things are still fresh."

Ross tells Mark that he has been taking notes on the consensus items and will send those notes to him tomorrow. He suggests that Mark ask Bill to document the consensus items reached today as well as remaining issues that will need further discussion after today's session in order to reach full consensus. He can distribute the notes as a draft document for Mark and the team to review, modify as necessary, and sign. If necessary, a review session, either in person or via teleconference, could be conducted to do further refinement of the wording and reach final consensus.

Mark nods his head in agreement. "Good idea," he says.

"Once the consensus document is finalized, you should create a PowerPoint presentation on the consensus items. The presentation can be used in the educational sessions that will be conducted for each of the divisions. The presentation should be simple and clear. Ideally, Jack should communicate it prior to the education sessions, and Bailey and you should be prepared to present it during the education sessions."

Mark has not projected far enough into the future to begin thinking about the education sessions in each division. He appreciates the experience that Ross brings to the project.

"That's a good plan," Mark comments. "I think Jack will be more than willing to send it out with a cover letter reinforcing why we're embarking on the IBP initiative. Coming from Jack will reinforce that Jack is the driver behind this effort."

Ross looks at his watch. "Time to reconvene," he says.

"I'd like to kick off this next session, if I may," Mark states.

"No problem," Ross says as they walk to the front of the room. Ross takes a seat on his stool while Mark calls the team to attention.

"Before we discuss implementation, I want to talk a little more about consensus and moving forward from this meeting. Ross and I had a conversation during the break, and here is what I propose we do."

He tells the group to speak up if there are any issues or items discussed today that remain areas of concern. He expects to have the usual change management issues in each division, to varying degrees. While these issues are very important, they do not need to be discussed today. The team's focus today should be on concerns relative to the concepts of Integrated Business Planning.

"If you do not raise concerns today, it will tell me that you are fully supportive of what has been discussed today. Silence will be considered acceptance," Mark says, as he looks each team member in the eyes.

Mark reviews the plan he and Ross discussed during the break for documenting consensus that was achieved today and other issues that need further discussion after today. He talks about the consensus presentation that will be developed.

"This presentation will be given to each of you to communicate to your individual teams and organizations. It will be a clear statement of objectives and directions from the central steering team," he explains. "It will help to provide a consistent message in company forums and during the education sessions. It will also be used by the educators and coaches from Effective Management, Inc."

Taylor speaks up, and Mark shoots Ross a glance. "We have covered a lot of ground today," he says. "Suppose after we've had a little more time to think, we have some differing thoughts or opinions from the consensus reached today? I don't want us to feel like we were railroaded into the consensus."

"Good point, Taylor," Mark replies. He reiterates that the decisions made today will be distributed to the team to review. That will be the team's opportunity to provide additional thoughts, gain clarity, and validate that there is consensus.

Mark glances around the room. "If you have issues or concerns, first of all, let me know. We will address them. I don't expect we will seek final consensus for a couple of weeks, so you will have a little soak time. And feel free to contact Ross with any questions or concerns."

Ross stands and walks toward Taylor. He explains to him and the team that one reason to use outside coaching is to have someone outside the company to discuss issues or concerns without fear of wasting internal people's time or appearing to not be supportive.

"That's our job," Ross says. "Bring questions and challenges to me, and I will address them directly or figure out a way to get you answers or get the issues addressed. For example, Taylor, I expect that you will have concerns on strategic integration and perhaps how to conduct a Strategic Review in the divisions. This is something new for much of Global Products, Inc. We can discuss this before the final consensus document is signed if that helps you."

"That would be very helpful. Thanks," Taylor replies.

Mark looks toward Bill. "Are you okay with documenting the consensus items and outstanding issues to be addressed? I expect that you would lead finalizing the consensus document once everyone has provided their comments and feedback," Mark asks.

"Got it," Bill replies. "I figured that would be one of my roles. I have been keeping a solid set of notes, so I am sure that, with Ross's review and help, we can get a draft to the team quickly."

Mark looks at each team member. No one speaks. Mark turns to Ross. "Okay, Ross. Let's move on to implementation."

Bill, now formally responsible for note taking, waves his hand and says, "Wait! Let me see if I captured our consensus on the IBP model before we go into implementation."

"Go ahead," Mark says.

"Let me read to the group what I documented," Bill says.

Taking a deep breath, he says, "Here goes."

Bill reads to the group from his notes:

"Since the time Global Products originally implemented Sales and Operations Planning, the process has continued to evolve and mature. Today, best practice is to use this integrated management process as the primary process to run the business. This more mature process is being called Integrated Business Planning to differentiate it from a more traditional Sales and Operations Planning process that is primarily focused on simple demand and supply balancing. Global Products' S&OP improvement project is really a project to implement Integrated Business Planning."

Bill looks up from his notes to make sure the team is tracking with his description of Integrated Business Planning. He resumes reading from his notes:

"The scope of this project is represented by the Integrated Business Planning model developed by Effective Management, Inc. This will become Global Products' implementation model. It includes the traditional S&OP model with the Product Management Review, Demand Review, Supply Review, Financial Appraisal, Integrated Reconciliation, and the Management Business Review.

"Implementation will take place within each division and will incorporate strategic management and business support functions (infrastructure/administration). The output of Integrated Business Planning will be connected to execution, via Master Supply Planning and Scheduling. As a result, connecting to Master Planning and Scheduling is within the scope of the Integrated Business Planning project, and Mark and Bailey will jointly own the project of integration from aggregate to detail and vice versa."

Bill pauses and looks up at the group again. The group is silent. He continues reading from his notes:

"The central steering committee is not mandating that the Integrated Business Planning model developed by Effective Management, Inc. be blindly followed. Rather, our direction is to incorporate all elements of Integrated Business Planning into an effective and efficient process. Each division's process structure will specifically address all the Integrated Business Planning elements in the appropriate sequence. The divisional process structure will be specifically addressed in process design where clear accountability for the process reviews will be established. The design of the individual business unit process steps will be part of the individual implementation plans of each business division."

Mark is grateful and pleased that Bill took the initiative to take notes on the consensus decisions.

"Excellent, Bill," Mark says. "Does anyone have comments, changes, or disagreements?"

The group is quiet. "Okay, then. Silence is acceptance. Now let's move on to implementation."

As Mark moves to the front of the room, Nolan calls out, "I have one quick question. Mark and Bailey have clarified their roles, and I assume, Ross, that you are supportive of those roles."

"Yes, Nolan. I am," Ross replies.

Nolan is not yet ready to move on. "One more thing. During the discussion on the Diamond, you talked briefly about Master Supply Planning and Scheduling. I am familiar with Master Supply Planning and Scheduling from a perspective of Supply Chain Management, and I recognize both the importance and the nuances in that application. In thinking about our discussions today, we are going to need similar processes and tools for the non-supply chain areas. Is there a set of tools out there that you recommend?"

Ross is pleased with the question, but hesitates to give any specific advice in this setting.

"Nolan, this is a very good question. The short answer is yes, and the tools come in different forms, such as project management tools for product development and innovation. Tools to support administrative functions often are oriented around specific tasks and due dates. Tools also exist for managing Human Resources. Your question deserves a longer discussion that is out of scope for today's session. Would you agree to my taking an action item to facilitate further discussion on non-supply chain functions?

"Sounds good," Nolan replies.

Bill's fingers tap lightly on his laptop keyboard as he documents the action item.

IMPLEMENTATION

WITHOUT FANFARE, ROSS DISPLAYS AN implementation model known as the Proven Path. (See Figure 30.) He always worries whether the detail is difficult to read, but the group does not seem to be struggling.

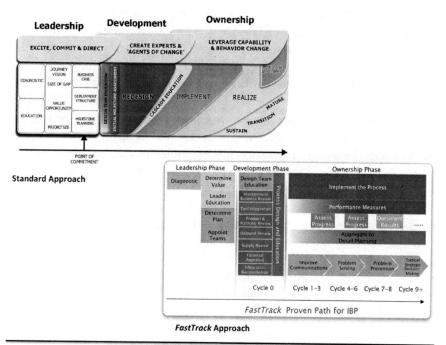

Figure 30   Proven Path Implementation Model (Copyright Oliver Wight International. Reproduced with permission.)

Nolan looks at the model in the class notebook, rather than the projector screen. He pushes the notebook away and whispers to Taylor, "Looks familiar."

"You're right, Nolan," Ross replies. "All of you have been exposed to this visual through the previous Proven Path implementations of S&OP. Am I correct?"

Everyone around the table nod their heads.

"That will help to jumpstart our discussion on implementation," Ross says. "What we will be looking to accomplish in this discussion is to reach consensus on using the Proven Path implementation approach for improving the current Sales and Operations Planning process and evolving and maturing it into Integrated Business Planning.

"I've got a question," Bill says. "The Proven Path worked for the initial S&OP implementation. Does it also work for an improvement project?"

"Yes, it does," Ross responds. "It serves as a framework for process improvement when the improvements are focused on improving S&OP or the improvements are focused on transitioning to IBP. Let me share my thoughts on how Global Products might want to move forward with the implementation. Then let's discuss your thoughts on the implementation."

Ross reiterates to the team that the improvements will be implemented at the individual division level, which means that each division will have its own project, project team, and project plan and schedule. It is expected that each division will be at different levels of maturity in the Sales and Operations Planning process. As a result, the specific improvements necessary to evolve to IBP will vary by division.

Bailey interrupts. "For companies with centralized management or centralized standardization, would you be taking a different approach?"

"We would still use the Proven Path implementation approach, but there may be a larger, central design team composed of division representatives instead of a small central steering committee like here at Global Products," Ross explains. "In a centralized management structure, each division would likely implement individually to a prescriptive design framework, predetermined by the central design team. This approach could create tighter boundaries that each division will be expected to follow."

"Don't we need some standardization in Global Products? I don't want to have to support an unnecessary number of software packages," Nolan says.

Before Ross can respond, Janis adds, "And I want an easy roll-up of financial numbers as well."

"That is exactly why both Finance and IT are on the central steering committee and were invited here today," Ross replies. "You should standardize wherever it makes sense to do so without imposing more rules than necessary."

Almost simultaneously in one voice, Mark and Bailey say, "We want ownership at the division level." They look at each other and chuckle.

"We can say you are aligned on that subject," Ross comments.

"But what about standardizing processes?" Taylor asks. "Isn't that a good idea? We want to use best practices whenever we can."

"That is why we have hired Effective Management, Inc.," Mark says. "They bring industry experience and their knowledge of how best practices have been deployed by other companies. They will be working with each of the divisions, which will make it easier to standardize wherever it makes sense. I am relying on Ross to do that for both Bailey and me. This approach worked well when we initially implemented S&OP."

"I agree with Mark," Ross says.

Ross explains that part of his job is to make sure that the central team has visibility of what is happening in the divisions and to ask for policy direction when a key area requires standardization or central direction. He also explains why it is important that the consensus from today's session is clearly articulated and signed by Jack, Mark, and Bailey."

"Let me state what I think I've heard," Janis says. "We, as the central steering committee, will determine areas that require standardization. At the same time, our implementation approach will be to make sure there is ownership at the division level for process improvement, for moving through all four stages of maturation, and for delivering the anticipated business results. Right?"

"Well stated!" Mark replies.

"How do we determine the anticipated business results?" Bailey asks.

Ross points to the Proven Path chart projected on the screen. He aims the laser pointer at the box labeled Value Opportunity. This is where the division _determines the potential value_ of the improvements.

He turns to the group and explains each division will be expected, with some coaching, to determine the anticipated results from the improvement effort. Each division will be provided reference information on the results other companies have achieved. Each division will also have the aid of a benefits model calculator to help identify the benefit opportunities for each business unit. The findings from the diagnostic will also provide input on the operational and financial improvement opportunities in each division. And they will know the areas of opportunity as a result of their individual division diagnostic. Since each division is already operating a Sales and Operations Planning process, the forward-looking projections reviewed each month should include the anticipated benefits from the improvement efforts.

"Thanks, Ross," Bailey says. "I'm comfortable with the approach for determining potential benefits. But Ross, your visual shows two Proven Paths. What are you trying to show?"

Ross responds quickly. "Thanks, Bailey. If you will give me a few more minutes, I will answer your question."

Ross asks the team to find the worksheet in their handout materials labeled Guidepost of Typical Benefits Achieved. (See Figure 31.) This worksheet is intended to help each division think about the sources of anticipated benefits. In each area of benefit in the worksheet, typical ranges of improvements that other companies have achieved are provided as a guidepost. The range of improvements has been documented by Effective Management, Inc.'s clients and in results reported in independent surveys conducted by research firms.

Bill is sitting on the edge of his seat. He obviously has a question that he is eager to have answered.

"What makes the Proven Path different from other project plans?" he asks.

	Reported % Improvement Ranges	Baseline Measure	Satisfied With Performance? Yes/No	Desired % Improvement	Impact of Achieving Improvement
Revenue Growth	10-31%				
Gross Margin	25-29%				
Demand Plan Accuracy	18-43%				
On-Time Delivery In Full	10-50%				
Order Fill Rate	29-34%				
Perfect Order	22-30%				
Customer Satisfaction	29-39%				
Inventory Turns	24-28%				
Inventory Value	33-37%				
Inventory Reduction	18-46%				
Safety Stock Reduction	11-45%				
Working Capital	25-30%				
Asset Utilization	32-49%				
Increased Productivity	30-45%				
Return on Assets	24-30%				

Figure 31 Guidepost of Typical Benefits Achieved
(Copyright Oliver Wight International. Reproduced with permission.)

"You may recall that the reason we call this approach the Proven Path is that it has been shown to work time and time again," Ross says.

He tells the group that the Proven Path implementation methodology is so named because it is proven. In the experience of Effective Management, Inc., when a company follows the steps in the Proven Path, the company is almost always successful.

Ross goes on to explain that, for Integrated Business Planning, it is recommended that the process is implemented as quickly as practical. When the Proven Path is used to implement quickly, time to results is shortened. This second Proven Path model on the visual is called the FastTrack Proven Path. It is designed to deliver results more quickly than any approach Effective Management, Inc. has utilized before, when the initiative being implemented is IBP.

"We have found that *time to results* is key to a successful, sustainable IBP implementation," Ross comments.

Mark turns to the team and explains that he and Jack did some independent research before today's session. They found that the longer it takes for an Integrated Business Planning project to be completed, the greater the chance for failure. It also costs more. This research endorses the Proven Path approach, especially the FastTrack Proven Path methodology. It is quicker, and quicker is better.

Ross advances the PowerPoint presentation to move the discussion to the main characteristics of the FastTrack Proven Path approach. "Here are the key characteristics of the Proven Path," he says, aiming the laser pointer at the screen. (See Figure 32.)

1. Since the project plan is specifically to transition Sales and Operations Planning to Integrated Business Planning, the elements of the project plan are pre-determined; little discovery is necessary.

2. In order to shorten the time to implement and make it easier for the implementation team, dedicated coaching is provided for each review in the Integrated Business Planning process. No person goes without experienced support. This support is provided by Effective Management, Inc.

3. Because the coaches all have previous subject matter experience and each function of the company has a coach, issues can be addressed quickly without being hampered by internal politics and historical sacred cows.

4. The implementation uses proven best practices, which means that discovery is not needed to determine the best practices. Knowledge of best practices is provided by Effective Management, Inc.'s coaches.

5. The people doing the process design are the people who will operate the new process or make the process changes.

Figure 32 Main Characteristics of the *FastTrack* Proven Path Implementation Methodology (Copyright Oliver Wight International. Reproduced with permission.)

Ross walks up to the projector screen and taps item number 5. "Let me repeat the fifth point again," he says. "The people doing the design are the people who will operate the new process or make the process changes."

"Let me reinforce Ross's point," Mark says.

He tells the group that having the business users design the process in the earlier Sales and Operations Planning implementations was a critical success factor. The company did not struggle with people taking ownership for the process. The business users were able to develop the designs more quickly and make needed changes to existing processes. As operators of the processes, they understood the details of the processes well, far better than an outside party.

"Our business users bring internal expertise on the nuances of our company's business model and business processes. Effective Management brings the knowledge of best practices. It dramatically shortens the time to results," Mark says.

"You're right, Mark," Janis says. "In the S&OP implementation, even though some people felt time pressures of doing their regular jobs and participating in the education and process design workshops, we had an operable S&OP process in just a few months. It wasn't perfect, but we saw results from the process right away."

Bill, the newcomer, asks: "Did we share findings and learnings between divisions?"

Ross explains that one of the advantages that large multi-divisional companies have over single-division companies is that the divisions can learn from one another. They can also take advantage of the other divisions' work.

"As project coordinator, Bill, you will want to help each division take advantage of the others' work whenever practical. The Effective Management coaches will do the same," Ross says.

Ross walks over to Janis and Taylor and places his hands on their shoulders. They have been animatedly whispering to one another. "Would you like to share with the group?" he asks.

They look up, with guilty expressions on their faces. "We are discussing whether there should be representatives from each division on the central steering team."

Ross decides to let Janis run with the thought. He came to greatly respect her as a leader in the previous Sales and Operations Planning implementations and knows that she will come to the right conclusion.

"And what did you conclude?" he asks.

"We know project leaders will be appointed in each division. We think they should be on the central steering team. That way, they can keep all of the divisions up to date on progress being made in each individual division. They can also provide input in decisions that are made centrally, but implemented at the division level."

"Shouldn't the division project leaders be those who are now the S&OP coordinators/leads in each division?" Nolan asks.

Mark responds before Ross can do so. "They are likely candidates but, remember, the S&OP coordinators/leads may have been appointed with a bias toward Supply Chain Management rather than company management. We'll need to carefully select the divisional IBP leaders, given that we are transitioning into Integrated Business Planning. We shouldn't automatically assume that the current S&OP coordinator will fulfill the role of IBP leader."

"Who decides?" Taylor asks.

Janis is quick to respond. "The division leader or, as Ross says, the Person In Charge," she replies.

Mark adds, "I assume the division leaders will solicit input from their direct reports."

"The S&OP coordinator for Universal Products division has a strategic management background. She is an example of a good candidate for the IBP leader," Janis says. "She's well regarded and reports high enough in the organization to have the ears of the division leadership team."

"I will personally make sure that the individual is high enough in the organization to be effective," Mark says. "Janis is correct. The IBP leader can't be just anyone who happens to be available. If there is an issue with regard to appointing the right individuals as IBP leaders, Jack Baxter has offered to step in if needed."

Ross is pleased with the discussion. Their concern about creating a strong, central team and appointing the right people to serve as IBP leaders shows the team's commitment to making the transition to IBP successful.

Bill has the success of the implementation on his mind as well. As if he is thinking out loud, he says, "It seems to me that, as each division works to improve each review process and the detailed processes that feed each review, the divisions will be developing internal subject matter experts. Wouldn't it be a good idea for functional teams across the divisions to share their learnings and best practices with each other? That way, they can learn from each other during the implementation and can continue to learn from each other after the implementation. That's what makes processes sustainable."

"Once the teams have been assigned, we encourage our clients to do just that," says Ross.

He tells the group that they should have the objective not only to develop subject matter experts who are knowledgeable about industry best practices for Integrated Business Planning but, also, to be knowledgeable on how those best practices are applied at Global Products. This approach is key to ensuring sustainability and continuous improvement of the processes. As the Integrated Business Planning processes mature, the focus of process leaders should shift to sustaining and improving the specific processes, not just in each division, but also across Global Products.

Ross picks up the remote control and advances the presentation to the next slide. "Take a look at this visual," he says. (See Figure 33.)

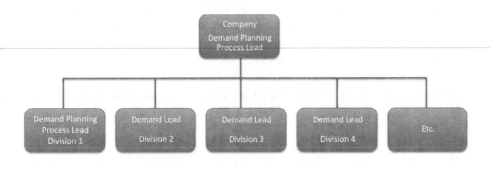

Figure 33 Structure for Sharing Learnings Across Businesses or Divisions
(Copyright Oliver Wight International. Reproduced with permission.)

Ross explains that the visual depicts a model of how subject matter experts from each division can work together to share learnings and collaborate on resolving issues. He tells the group it is premature, at this point, to determine how cross-divisional teams will collaborate. The question should be addressed in four to six months after the new foundation of Integrated Business Planning has been established in each division.

The project team continues to discuss details of each phase of the Proven Path implementation. (See Figure 30.) They reach consensus on implementation activities and responsibilities, which Bill dutifully documents.

Around 4:30 pm, the conversation dwindles to a halt.

Ross scans the group. The team members are obviously tired.

"Are there any more implementation issues you would like to discuss?"

Everyone shakes his or her head "No".

The ring of the telephone console in the center of the table shatters the silence. Janis reaches out and presses the answer button on the phone.

"Hello?" she says.

"How has the day gone?"

It is Jack calling from Japan.

"Good morning, Jack," Mark says. "We're winding up a good day here, just as you are starting the morning in Japan."

"Have you discussed implementation yet?" Jack asks.

"Yes," the group responds in unison.

"Are there any obstacles to a FastTrack Proven Path approach?" Jack asks.

"No," the group says in unison.

"Good," Jack says. "We are faced with challenges of growth when the market dynamics are changing and seem to be more volatile. We need greater cross-functional alignment going forward in order to better execute our strategies. I want to improve our process and transition it to Integrated Business Planning. And the sooner we do so, the better, given what I'm seeing with the market dynamics."

"You won't get any arguments from us on that point," Mark says.

"We're ready to roll," Janis chimes in.

The rest of the team members say, "Yes!"

"I'm glad to hear it," Jack replies. "I'll look forward to reviewing the implementation plans when I get back. But don't wait for my return to get started."

GETTING STARTED

THE TEAM DOES NOT WAIT for Jack to return before taking the first steps to begin the project to improve the Sales and Operations Planning process by transitioning it to Integrated Business Planning. Bill and Ross meet the following Monday to review the consensus document before sending it for Mark's review.

Mark makes a few changes to add clarity before distributing the document to the team members for their review. He leads a teleconference three days later to review and agree upon the final changes that have been submitted by the team members. The team also reviews and agrees upon a PowerPoint presentation for the business leaders of each division to present, explaining Integrated Business Planning, why it is being implemented, and what to expect from the process.

When Jack returns from Japan the next day, he is presented with a letter for his signature that is a directive about Integrated Business Planning. Mark and Bailey have already signed the letter. It will be sent to the business leaders of each business division to circulate throughout the division.

"The letter is good," Jack says, as he places his pen in his shirt pocket after signing the document. "I hope you don't mind, but I'm going to personally call the division leaders, too. I want to be sure it is crystal clear that Integrated Business Planning is a key initiative, and I expect each division to embrace it fully. I want them to know that I expect visible, measureable results within six months."

Mark, Bill, and Ross nod in agreement.

"Before you go, let's talk a moment about how we're going to document the results," Jack says.

Mark recalls that the divisions that were most successful in implementing Sales and Operations Planning eight years ago made it a point to keep track of the benefits received from implementing the process.

Jack reminds the group that some of the benefits, like inventory reduction and reduced costs, will be easily measureable. Other benefits will be more difficult to quantify but, in the end, will be more important than the operational improvements. He also reminds Mark not to forget to document costs avoided, which were significant in the early phase of implementation eight years ago. Finally, he tells Mark that he expects to see qualitative benefits, such as improved trust, better communications, stronger teamwork among the divisional leadership team members, more available management and leadership time, and ease of transferring key talent between divisions.

"Remember, with S&OP, each division utilized the same basic management process in which accountabilities were clearly defined. This structure reduced the time to effectiveness when people were transferred or promoted," he reminds his team.

"We also shifted to more strategic thinking, which, in my opinion, helped us to make better business decisions," Jack says. "It's hard to measure and quantify improved decision making. But I know it when I see it."

"So true," Ross agrees. "Don't forget quality of life. It is also hard to measure, but is one of the biggest 'soft' benefits. A company that is under control, even in difficult economic times, has a different environment than a company that is not under control. It is a less stressful, less chaotic, more rewarding place to work. Real business problems still exist, but at least people get to spend their time on real problems instead of on self-inflicted, internally generated issues."

"Our people will say that, with S&OP, they gained more discretionary time at work to spend on business growth and improvements," Mark recollects. "They also gained more time away from work to spend with their family and loved ones."

"Integrated Business Planning should improve upon those previous results," Jack says. "And it will touch all of our business functions. And we should become more adept at executing our strategies. I hope my expectations are clear."

Mark, Bob, and Ross nod their heads in agreement.

Mark clasps Ross on the shoulder. "Let me walk you out, Ross," he says.

Mark and Ross shake hands in the lobby. The diagnostics, education, and design sessions are being scheduled, and Ross promises to make sure the instructors from Effective Management, Inc. are working with the local division leaders to coordinate the sessions.

"I'm optimistic," Ross says. "That does not mean that the transition to Integrated Business Planning won't have its challenges, but Global Products has one large advantage, Mark, and that's the quality of your people. They will get the job done."

It is eighteen months later. Integrated Business Planning is operating effectively in all divisions of Global Products, Inc.

Jack Baxter, President of Global Products and Services, has just wrapped up a session with the implementation team. He recognized their accomplishment in implementing both Integrated Business Planning and Master Supply Planning and Scheduling. He also highlighted the measurable results that have been achieved in each division.

Jack and his team are now in the cafeteria enjoying lunch with Ross. Mark Ryan, a division General Manager, and Bailey Madison, Vice President of Supply Chain Management, sit side by side, trading jibes about the experience in implementing Integrated Business Planning and Master Supply Planning and Scheduling simultaneously and successfully.

"Jack, in spurring us to action, you spoke about market volatility. What an understatement," Janis Novak, the Controller for Universal Products, remarks.

"The Great Recession jolted us. That's for sure," Jack replies.

"Global Products has done better than many businesses during and coming out of the recession," observes Ross Peterson, their coach and educator from Effective Management, Inc.

"We have two fewer competitors, and we're buying the assets of one of those competitors," Janis says.

"We have the persistence of Tim Osborne and the cross-divisional demand team to thank for being ahead of the curve on both the downturn and now the upturn," Jack says.

At that moment, Tim strides past the table, carrying a tray of food. Jack greets Tim, and they shake hands.

"Join us," Jack says. "We were just talking about you and the other Demand Planning leaders. If it wasn't for your persistence, we would not have responded to the downturn."

Tim smiles at the group. He recalls the difficulty he had in getting the leadership team to acknowledge that the recession was going to hit Global Products full force. For two months during the Management Business Reviews, the leadership teams asked for more information about the demand projections and the economic assumptions.

"I was very frustrated," Tim says, "But it was a valuable lesson. The first month, I drowned you with data. The second month, we got the demand leaders together from each division and shared what we were seeing in the marketplace. We put together several scenarios and documented the assumptions for each scenario. Then we tracked the assumptions. In the end, deciding which scenario to choose was not controversial at all."

Jack chuckles. "As I recall, it was the worst-case scenario."

"That is true, but it sure saved our you-know-whats," Bailey says. "We were able to draw down inventory; and not just finished goods, but raw material, too."

"Which gave us a stronger cash position," Janis continues the story. "When Wannamaker closed their doors, we had the cash to buy their assets."

"We also thought strategically about how we wanted to shape the market and supply chain," recalls Taylor Jackson, Vice President of Strategy for Global Products and Services. "The cash came in handy to help out our strategic suppliers. We also made some good decisions on where to invest in new products."

Jack leans back in his chair and places his hands over his head. "What I'd like to know, Tim, is how you predicted the upturn so well?"

"It helps to have a team," Tim says. "All of the divisions' demand coordinators met every month after each Management Business Review. We shared what we learned about market conditions and agreed on the indicators we should follow. Each demand coordinator was responsible for reporting changes to certain indicators. We began creating scenarios for the upturn, but we really could not predict the timing with any confidence. We knew business would improve, but not exactly when."

"We couldn't have made the decision to add shifts and begin to build finished goods inventory without those scenarios," Mark observes. "The information you brought to the table gave us the confidence to take some risks, like building inventory and hiring people."

"Jack, you asked us to document hard benefits, and the results are quite good," Janis says. "Every division has increased market share, and our sales revenues are higher than we predicted. So the investment in increasing our capacity and inventory has paid off."

"We've been tracking express shipment costs," Bailey adds. "Compared to before the recession, we are now spending $800,000 to $1 million less each month."

"And we are in a position to acquire another business, which is part of our business strategy," Taylor adds.

"Remember my talking about the soft benefits of Integrated Business Planning?" Ross asks. "What you all have just described is collaborative teamwork."

"Which brought us good business decision making," Jack says. "I told you I would know good decision making when I saw it, and I have seen it. The recession helped to bring us together. Let's not stop this executive collaboration with the return of good times. The market will remain volatile, and our remaining competitors will scramble to catch up with us."

Mark slaps Jack on the shoulder. "I can't imagine running a business without Integrated Business Planning," he says.

"I can guarantee you that I never will," Janis says.

Ross looks at his watch and pushes away from the table. "It's time for me to go."

"Where do you fly tonight?" Mark asks.

"We're starting another Integrated Business Planning implementation at a company in Tulsa," Ross replies.

"I hope it's as successful as our implementation," Jack says as he shakes Ross's hand.

"I'll show myself out," Ross says, not wanting to break up the team's reminiscing.

As he walks down the hall toward the lobby, Ross shifts mental gears. He's thinking about the company in Tulsa. Their value proposition is heavily service oriented, and they don't do much manufacturing. Yet, they have all the same alignment and resource synchronization problems. The company has a strong leader, like Jack, and the management team is talented.

That's a good start, Ross thinks to himself, as he turns on the ignition in the car and heads to the airport.

Characteristics (People, Process, Tools)	Detail Planning Only	"Capable" S&OP Process	Integrated Business Planning Process	Mature Integrated Business Planning Process
Involvement	Middle management driven. Executive team not active or does not participate.	Executive team and middle management.	Senior executive driven and owned. Leadership and management operating as a company team.	Senior executive driven for continual improvement to the reliability of resulting plans and execution results. Achievement of business results.
Frequency	Daily or weekly	Monthly	Monthly and on demand as special needs occurs.	Monthly updating and alignment of all company plans. Plans can be updated and re-aligned in special situations or significant emergencies within 1 to 5 days.
Planning Horizon	Short term -- end of month, next month, and the current quarter.	24 months rolling.	24+ months rolling; quarterly rolling for beyond 2 years. Strategic goals quantified in out years.	Anticipated significant changes or uncertainties at any point in the planning horizon are addressed to ensure decisions are made in time for execution without panic.

Appendix Detailed Planning, S&OP and IBP – There Is a Difference
(Copyright Oliver Wight International. Reproduced with permission.)

Characteristics (People, Process, Tools)	Detail Planning Only	"Capable" S&OP Process	Integrated Business Planning Process	Mature Integrated Business Planning Process
Focus	Historical focus and within short detail planning time fence.	3 months and beyond to better communicate and solve and prevent problems.	3 months and beyond to have sufficient time to prevent problems, exploit opportunities, and mitigate risks.	Scenarios are developed for any portion of the planning horizon to better understand uncertainty, risk and opportunities that have a high impact on business performance.
Language	Volume: SKU or detail for production plan and forecast.	Volume, revenue, and margin: Product families and sub-families.	Volume, revenue, and margin: Assumptions, families, channels, segments, and product lines. Scenario development is the norm.	Corporate performance management in executing the business goals and strategies and performing reliably. Sarbanes-Oxley compliance is routine with little risk of non-compliance.
Integration	Supply/demand balancing and inventory planning. Many unexpected internal surprises - reactionary in nature.	Gap-closing plans and their financial impact for demand, supply, and inventory to meet annual business plan expectations.	Gap-closing plans for demand, supply, inventory, product portfolio, and financial performance to achieve business plan and strategy.	Business and strategic planning are no longer significant annual events. Focus has shifted to continuous review and adaptation. Focus of annual business and strategic planning is for multi-year goal setting and to revisit corporate vision and mission.

Appendix Detailed Planning, S&OP and IBP – There Is a Difference (Continued)
(Copyright Oliver Wight International. Reproduced with permission.)

Characteristics (People, Process, Tools)	Detail Planning Only	"Capable" S&OP Process	Integrated Business Planning Process	Mature Integrated Business Planning Process
Modeling	Supply Chain centric. Some or no production capacity planning. Rules of thumb and ad-hoc policy. Little supply chain optimization.	Resource planning of critical or constrained production centers or equipment and key suppliers.	Resource planning of critical assets -- equipment, product development capability, facilities, people, and financial capability. Multiple scenarios are developed.	What-if scenario planning to determine the most advantageous response to opportunity, uncertainty, risks, and market dynamics.
Strategy	Robust strategies are missing or are not considered in the process.	Some focus on strategic projects primarily involving supply and demand capability. Supply Chain strategy complements the Business Strategy.	Focus on deployment of strategy and identifying when current strategies need to change. Rigor in alignment of Product Portfolio management.	Monthly strategy execution reviews and adjustments as needed.
Finance	Little financial information. Financials developed independent from the process.	Price, cost, inventory, and margin projections. Income statement, balance sheet and cash flow available.	Monthly updates of projected income statement, cash, capital, activity-based costing, which simplifies the annual business planning process.	Flexible budgeting with annual business planning no longer a significant event.
Decisions	Demand/supply balancing decisions impacting short-term execution and customer service.	Tactical decisions for resolving demand, supply, and inventory issues anticipated over the mid- and long-term.	Tactical and strategic decisions impacting product portfolio management, demand management, supply management, and financial management.	Continuous tactical and strategic reviews to ensure alignment of all corporate plans and activities to attain the business goals and strategies.

Appendix Detailed Planning, S&OP and IBP – There Is a Difference (Continued)
(Copyright Oliver Wight International. Reproduced with permission.)

Characteristics (People, Process, Tools)	Detail Planning Only	"Capable" S&OP Process	Integrated Business Planning Process	Mature Integrated Business Planning Process
Teamwork and Behavior	Functional focus in demand and supply organizations often with frequent adversarial situations.	Team-based management is established: Conscious drive to company, not functional, awareness with common agenda and goals. Management Business Review decision making outside the S&OP process is not allowed.	Unconscious competence in team-based management. It is natural to believe and act in the company interest.	Trust, respect, transparency, openness, and honesty are organizational values. Misbehavior is rare. Performance management is focused on cross-functional collaboration to achieve the business plan and strategy.
Outcome	Near-term production plan and demand control.	Alignment of demand, supply, and inventory plans at the aggregate level. Financial gaps identified.	Alignment of all corporate plans at the aggregate level with a focus on the actions required to execute the company business and strategic plan.	Aggregate plans are routinely reviewed and realigned as needed. Company is demand driven with the capability to exploit opportunities in the market place and effectively respond to change in the marketplace.

Appendix Detailed Planning, S&OP and IBP – There Is a Difference (Continued)
(Copyright Oliver Wight International. Reproduced with permission.)

Lightning Source UK Ltd.
Milton Keynes UK
UKOW03n1028260713

214381UK00001B/1/P